Money Mind

Psychological Strategies
To Dominate Stock Market Investing

The Sick Economist

Disclaimer

No content published in this book constitutes a recommendation that any particular security, portfolio of securities, transaction or investment strategy is suitable for any specific person. You further understand that neither the author nor their affiliates are advising you personally concerning the nature, potential, value or suitability of any particular security, portfolio of securities, transaction, investment strategy or other matter. To the extent that any of the content published in this book may be deemed to be investment advice or recommendations in connection with a particular security, such information is impersonal and not tailored to the investment needs of any specific person. You understand that an investment in any security is subject to a number of risks, and that discussions of any security published in this book will not contain a list or description of relevant risk factors.

This book is not intended to provide tax, legal, insurance or investment advice, and nothing in the book should be construed as an offer to sell, a solicitation of an offer to buy, or a recommendation for any security by *The Sick Economist* or any third party. You alone are solely responsible for determining whether any investment, security or strategy, or any other product or service, is appropriate or suitable for you based on your investment objectives and personal and financial situation. You should consult an attorney or tax professional regarding your specific legal or tax situation.

This book is dedicated to those who raised me, those who raised them, and the pioneers who came before. Many generations of independent thinkers.

Acknowledgements

A heart felt "Thank You" to my informal brain trust, who have always been generous with their time and honest feedback:

BRH, DZR, the Notorious Professor S, the Wolfman, and Ryan M.

Contents

Introduction: Why I Wrote This Book, and How This Book Can Help You

I had to write this book because the same thing happens every time. It. Happens. Every. Time. It could be because the Stock Market has had a big swing up or a big swing down; some kind of major political or even historical event may have occurred that seems as if it will affect stock prices. Or it could be that a friend of mine just experienced a major life event, like the birth of a child or the death of a parent. Or it could simply be because it's 3:00 PM on a Tuesday, someone felt anxious or bored on that day.

My phone rings. My friend speaks first. The conversation typically goes like this:

"Man, can you believe that market today! Down 3%! What should I do? Should I be selling?"

I would almost always reply like this. "Do you have a well balanced portfolio of different stocks, say at least ten different stocks?"

"Yes."

"Do you need the money right away for some kind of emergency?"

"No."

"Ok, then, just do nothing. Study after study demonstrates that 'buy and hold' is the way to go. Relax, go play golf or something. The market goes up and down … it's no big deal."

"Yes, yes, I know … but I should be doing something, shouldn't I? Maybe I should just sell half my stocks."

"No, really, just go play golf."

"Maybe I'll just sell 10% and then, when the market goes down, I will buy more."

"You could, but really, just go play golf."

"If the market is going down for X or Y reason, maybe I should be shorting stocks?"

"No, probably not necessary. Trust me, the market does quite well over time ..."

"You're right. You're right. So I should be buying? Maybe I should borrow money and buy even more?"

"Please don't. Just buy a little here and there and spend the rest of the time on your boat."

"All together, I heard the real money is in options. Maybe I should be using stock options to protect my gains and stop losses. I heard that's what the pros do."

"You're not a pro, and, believe me, even the pros often get it wrong. Just go to the beach today, it's nice outside."

"Go to the beach? There is money to be made in this market! My friend's cousin told him that this hot tech stock, xyz inc. is set to triple. He said it's a lock. Shouldn't I be buying that?"

"Please. Go. To. The Beach. Leave your computer at home."

"God, this stock game is so complicated. No wonder the pros make all the money. What would you do?"

"I would do nothing. Stick with the stocks I have. Occasionally buy more if I can. Then go enjoy my life. Any chance you will follow this advice?"

"Yeah, sure, I know you must be right. Just buy and hold. Ok, good. Thanks for talking."

End of the conversation, but never the end of the ordeal. Almost always the same guy calls me up a month later, a year later, or even ten years later, and announces that he lost too much money in the market. It's too complicated, he tried everything, and from now on, he's just going to invest in other things. This is how high-income professionals and entrepreneurs, people who make well into the six figures or beyond, make so much but keep so little. This is how high-performance professionals, people who have excelled and dominated in executive roles, wind up just scraping by in old age. They made a lot but kept very little.

I used to think that only poor people made dumb moves in the stock market. Afterall, the data show, again and again, that the US Stock Market has been an unparalleled profit-generating machine, year after year, decade after decade, for centuries. How could an educated professional, someone with above-average education and above-average income, somehow miss financial layups with alarming regularity?

Even a cursory glance at stock market research demonstrates that the behavior above is not unusual; in fact, it's the norm. According to a study published by the research organization DALBAR, as of 2017, the S&P 500, a broad basket of America's largest companies, returned 7.68% per year over the previous two decades. However, the average investor gained only 4.79%. To put that in real terms, an investor who invested $10,000 initially and then $500 a month every month for twenty years would have wound up with $308,954 after twenty years, if he bought the S&P 500 and never did anything. If the same investor, described in my phone conversation above, achieved the average returns described in the research literature, he would only have $219,540. So, what's the reward for the eternally vigilant and active investor? $100,000 less than if he had just played golf for twenty years. And, remember, these are just averages. That means that a lot of smart, educated, and generally successful people chronically lag the averages by more than 3% points. It could be anyone you know and respect. You might even recognize yourself in this group.

So, it's been mathematically proven, again and again, that buying and holding is the way to go for most investors. Very simple. So why does almost no one do this? As Warren Buffett, one of the world's most successful investors, is fond of saying, making big money in the stock market is "simple, but not easy."

The barriers to stock market riches are not intellectual. The barriers are not educational or even financial. The barriers to sustained long-term investment success are emotional. I know people with dazzling intellect and superior executive skills who are constantly losing their shirts in the market. They don't have the emotional toolkit to succeed.

That's what this book is all about. The goal of this book is to help you gain the emotional tools to ride out any storm in the Stock Market.

Some people are just born more patient and calmer than others, just like some people are born with a better genetic propensity to be muscular and buff. Your thoughts and feelings come from your brain, and your brain is a body part that can be trained, just like any other muscle in your body. If you doubt that this approach can work for you, try the following exercise:

Think of your favorite movie star. Go on the internet and type in "before he was famous."

You'd be amazed how many were just average schlubs before they "went Hollywood." Hollywood is famous for taking average-looking leading men (or women), putting them on a strict training routine, and turning them into lean, mean, Instagram photo op machines. The goal of this book is to do the same with your mind. The following chapters are filled with thought exercises that will make your self-control and patience just as buff as the Rock's legendary pecs and abs.

When you choose to invest in stocks, the successful investor learns to accept that there are many factors that she can't control. But she can control her mental attitude regarding her money, which will in turn control her actions and her outcomes.

The traditional saying is, "Mind over matter." I will teach you that when it comes to investing success, the saying should be "mind over money."

Market Timing - S&P 500 Returns Excluding Top Days

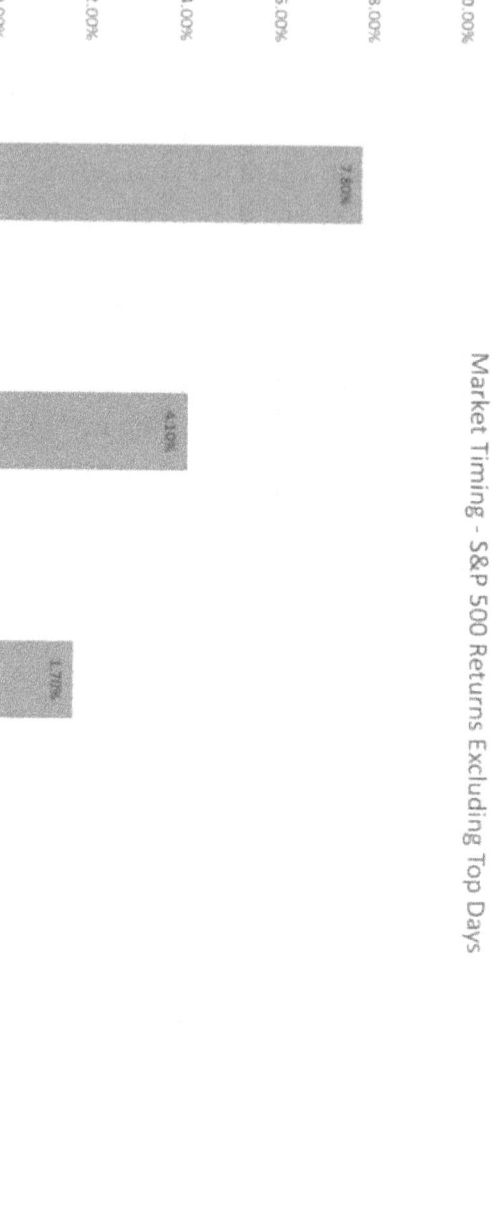

10.00%				
8.00%				
6.00%				
4.00%				
2.00%				
0.00%				
-2.00%				
-4.00%				

Total S&P 500 Index Annual Return: 7.80%
Excluding Top 10 Days: 4.10%
Excluding Top 20 Days: 1.70%
Excluding Top 30 Days: 0.40%
Excluding Top 40 Days: -2.30%

Data Provided By Schwab Center For Financial Research. Graphs &
Data Analysis by Lee Rivers. Colorado College. 2020.

Range of S&P 500 Returns (1926-2011)

Data Provided By Schwab Center For Financial Research. Graphs & Data Analysis by Lee Rivers, Colorado College, 2020.

7

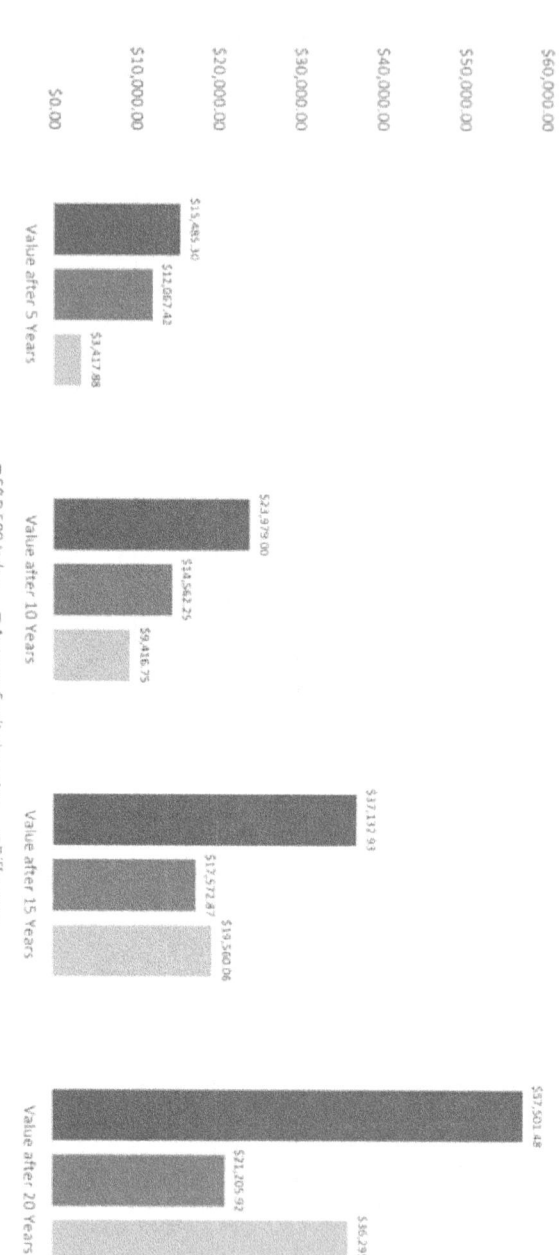

Return on $10,000 - S&P 500 Index vs Average Equity Investor

Data Provided By Schwab Center For Financial Research. Graphs & Data Analysis by Lee Rivers, Colorado College, 2020.

Chapter 1: Better Off Dead

Top executives that run Fidelity Investments, one of the largest wealth management firms in the world, ordered a private internal review of investors' accounts to see which kinds of investors do the best over time. If you have ever opened a brokerage account, you know that they ask all kinds of seemingly asinine questions when you fill out the initial paperwork. The reason they do that is so that they can track and measure data and 'get to know their customers'.

Based on the data that Fidelity had religiously collected over decades, and their very intimate knowledge of clients' investment outcomes, the wisemen running Fidelity decided to figure out who did best. Was it retired executives? Young punks who trade a lot? Stay-at-home moms who manage the family's finances?

None of those, actually. It turned out that the best accounts with the juiciest long-term returns were owned by dead people. That's right; your dead grandma outperformed a retired CFO or a kid with a Harvard MBA.

Sounds both terrible and great at the same time, doesn't it? How could all of those seasoned pros, with decades of business experience, be left in the dust by someone currently six feet under? On the other hand, if a corpse can do well, couldn't you also do well?

However, if you take the time to really research the authenticity of this story, it's tough to find hard evidence that this study ever really happened. Fidelity certainly doesn't admit to it.

But then again, why would they? They make money every time an investor trades, and they make money off active management and vigorous investment advice. "Buy and hold until you die" won't make money for Fidelity. So it's hard to prove that this story is 100% true. But it's child's play to prove that it's 100% true in terms of results and findings.

The Cold Hard Facts

It's debatable whether Fidelity ever conducted the above study, but many other credible institutions have. According to The Journal of Finance (Volume LV, #2) a team of Professors from the Haas School of Business at Berkeley, found that investors who traded the most, lost the most. This was a study involving 66,000 households. The households that were constantly buying and selling lagged the overall market indices by a whopping 6.5%. You will remember from the DALBAR study in the introduction; a difference of just 3% in annual performance equated to huge differences over time. Losing out by 6.5% is catastrophic.

The investigators at the Haas school of Business weren't the only ones to find this kind of data. In a study published in The Financial Analysts Journal, professors Douglas J. Jordan and J. David Dilitz utilized two different methods to analyze the profitability of a sample of 'day traders'. Day traders are a type of financial speculator who trade constantly in and out of stock positions, often relying on technical metrics and borrowed money. The authors found that, even when analyzed two different ways, 80% of the traders lost money consistently. Of the 20% who made money, the authors found substantial evidence that they only made money because the overall market was going up during the study period. In other words, the 20% that made money by trading heavily just got lucky.

These studies are only the tip of the iceberg. Research after research has found that more trading does not equal more profit. In fact, it's almost always an inverse relationship. He who trades most, loses most.

But what about our hypothetical dead man? Well, let's imagine a financial Rip Van Winkle. He's not so much dead, but simply 'asleep'. The well-known financial advisory firm, Raymond James, investigated this idea. Let's say you had invested $1 in a broad basket of large stocks in 1926. By 2010, that measly $1 would be worth $2,982. You could have been collecting stamps, exploring the Amazon, or just napping for 74 years. But you would have earned a 2900% return on your money while paying no attention at all. If you had chosen to invest the same $1 in a broad basket of smaller, lesser known stocks, your $1 would have multiplied to an astonishing $16,055! Not bad, considering you spent the last 74 years knitting blankets, flying kites, or studying interpretive dance.

The numbers are unequivocal and crystal clear; less is more when it comes to stock market investing.

Simple, But Not Easy

If study after study has employed simple arithmetic to demonstrate that 'buy and hold' is the best strategy, why do I keep getting phone calls like the one described in the Introduction? Why do rational, well-educated people turn into stark raving lunatics when it comes to stock market investing?

There are a few reasons for this; none of which have to do with pure math or rational self interest. Almost all have to do with feelings.

First of all, everything about American culture relates to action: taking action to make things happen. Think about the basic history lessons you were taught in grade school. Almost always, great men and women are introduced as what they did. George Washington led the Continental Army and founded America. Abraham Lincoln led the Union to victory in the Civil War and freed the slaves. Harriet Tubman escaped slavery and formed the Underground Railroad. We are, fundamentally, a nation of doers.

The same ethos expands to our pop culture references related to business, especially Wall Street and Big Business. Anyone between the age of forty and seventy remembers the character of Gordon Gekko from the movie "Wall Street." Slicked-back hair, suspenders, and a hell raising devil-may-care attitude. That was a man who made things happen. A doer.

Another reason why people feel they must do something to their stock portfolio on a regular basis is due to American ideals about work. It may seem like our Puritan founders are long-gone, buried, and forgotten, but their ethos remains embedded deeply in the psyche of many Americans. Our Puritan founders were obsessed with work and even associated work with ethical goodness and godliness. Even in today's more cynical and frustrated times, the majority of Americans would associate the phrase 'hard work' with 'The American Dream'. In America, 'good' people work hard.

Outsized financial returns with minimal or no work flies in the face of our most core American teachings. Therefore, many otherwise rational people feel compelled to make work when there is none. To most Americans, it just seems impossible to believe that they could invest $1, do absolutely nothing, and come back 74 years later to find that it had increased to $2,982. Someone must have done hard work to make that happen. Well, it turns out, someone did. But not the investor. The investor had everyone else working for him. We will go over this much more in depth in a later chapter.

Fear is also a big factor. Because most American investors also work in other capacities, they know the value of a dollar in an emotional sense. They work hard to achieve a decent (or better than decent) income and they put those hard-earned dollars to work in the stock market. When the market goes through one of its violent swoons, which it always will from time to time, it's just too much for those fearful investors. They worked so hard for that money! But it goes up, it goes down, it goes sideways ... it's nauseating.

If you were in a speeding car that suddenly started swerving all over the place, would you grab the wheel and try to regain control? Or would you just chill out as the car careened from side to side, serenely relaxing as the car almost spins off the road at 70 MPH?   The impulse of many fearful people is to grab control and do something. That may well be the right thing to do in a car, but with stocks, it's the dead wrong move.

So, we have a toxic stew of an action-oriented culture, a work-obsessed culture, and fear that isn't based on fact. Then, of course, we have the most fundamental of American ingredients; Capitalism.

Raymond James' study demonstrated that you could earn a 2900% return by just doing nothing. This was terrible news for Raymond James. Financial Advisory firms really only make money by rousing people to action. If you buy and hold, the only person who makes money is you. If you are constantly trading, everyone else makes more money. So which course of action do you think you will be guided towards?

It's true that there has been an evolution in the business of financial advice and that the industry has generally evolved to be less exploitative. However, most companies in the business of financial advice have something to sell, and doing nothing doesn't help your advisor buy a ski lodge in Montana.

For many years, the only way to buy and sell stocks was through a broker. This is an old-fashioned relationship. To buy shares in a company, one would call up the broker, who earned a commission for selling shares. Although generations of well-to-do individuals built up trusting working relationships with these brokers, the core incentives were still all wrong. Brokers made money by selling you stuff. More trading meant more commission for them. The results for the investor were barely relevant.

As we entered the '90s, the discount electronic brokerage was born. This was similar to the original concept of buying stocks through a broker, except instead of calling a broker, having an in-depth conversation, and paying a big commission on stock, one could pay a small commission and do the work themselves online. This may have reduced conflicts, but an online discount brokerage was still a brokerage; brokers still got commission based on the trades of their investors. More trading remained good for them and bad for the investor.

Lately, the online brokerage business has experienced new competitive pressure as young upstart brokerages have joined the fray. Trading commissions have actually fallen to $0. When it became 'free' to trade, trading went through the roof. Despite 10 different Harvard studies, no one seemed to care. With no obvious incentive not to trade, legions of wannabe Gordon Gekkos are currently furiously busy losing money or getting ready to lose money.

You may notice how I wrote 'free': Does anyone ever really do anything for free? Of course not. Online brokerages still make money when you trade, because there is a tiny markup on the securities you are buying from them. They're only making on average one penny per share (more or less), but with over tens or hundreds of millions of trades per day, it adds up. So what's the bottom line? Even with no obvious fees to the investor, the brokerages still want them to trade as much as possible. They make money that way.

I am not the only person who has noticed the obvious conflicts that arise from giving advice on a commission-based compensation plan. Over the last 20 years or so, we have seen the rise of fee-based advisors. These could be advisors that are paid by the hour (the way you would a lawyer) or, more commonly, paid with a fixed percentage of your assets (typically 0.5%–1.5%). This arrangement reduces the incentive for an investor to churn their account. The advisor gets paid the same whether the investor trades once a year or once a day and if the investor's account value shrinks, the advisor's fee is less.

This incentive system is better, but still not great for the investor. If they are not trading much, then what kind of advice are they paying for?

I recently had a wealthy friend that came to me and said, "I am paying 0.75% of my assets every year to just sit there. This fee adds up to over $10,000 a year. What am I paying for?"

In my friend's case, his very scrupulous advisor was actually dispensing wise counsel. However, many professional money managers fear exactly the conversation that I described, so they wind up feeling pressured to advise clients to take some kind of action. Studies from Berkeley or not, everybody has bills to pay, including your financial advisor.

The reasons for trading discussed here are just the tip of the iceberg. I have heard every bizarre reason why stocks just must be bought and sold, financing must be arranged, and options and complicated derivatives must be part of a portfolio. Not one of them holds up to math. But feelings are far more important than math any day of the week.

Be the Marshmallow Man

Every study utilizing a range of different techniques, completed by a wide range of different investigators, indicates that 'patience pays'. So be patient and make big money.

End of book, right?

No. Not even close. Anyone will tell you that patience pays. But they never seem to tell you how to be patient.

Super investor Warren Buffett is famous for aphorisms, such as, "If you can't own a stock for ten years, then you shouldn't own it for ten minutes." He has said dozens of these kinds of quotations. But notice that he never tells you how to be patient. Most people assume that a person either is patient and calm or isn't, just like a person is tall or isn't. But, once again, we have a wealth of studies and data that indicate just the opposite.

One of the most famous of these studies is the Stanford Marshmallow experiment. This study was first conducted in 1972 by the famous psychologist, Dr. Walter Mischel. The study was very simple. A kindergarten-aged child was offered a treat (typically a marshmallow) and given a choice. They were told that they could either eat the marshmallow on the spot and enjoy it, or they could wait fifteen minutes and they would get two marshmallows. The researcher would leave the room, with the marshmallow sitting on a plate in front of the child, and allow the child to decide for themselves.

Most of the children gobbled up the marshmallow immediately. However, a significant minority of the children waited for the researcher to return. They wanted those two marshmallows and were willing to do what they needed to get them. The progress of those children was then followed through adulthood. Guess which group had much more successful lives? (As measured by SAT scores, educational attainment, body weight, and other common measurements). Of course, the more patient children did much better over time. Mini Warren Buffetts, each of them.

The end results were not the most relevant findings, but rather that each child employed different techniques to delay gratification.

When describing the behavior of the children, the researchers explained that "They made up quiet songs ... hid their heads in their arms, pounded the floor with their feet, fiddled playfully and teasingly with the signal bell, verbalized the contingency, prayed to the ceiling, and so on. In one dramatically effective self-distraction technique, after obviously experiencing much agitation, a little girl rested her head, sat limply, relaxed herself, and proceeded to fall sound asleep."

It wasn't easy to resist the temptation of that sweet marshmallow, but some of the tykes pulled it off. They used tools and tactics to remain patient. Their successful patience didn't just come naturally.

So, if Warren Buffett can praise the virtues of patience when it comes to investing, why doesn't he explain how he does it? "The stock market is a device for transferring money from the impatient to the patient." Thanks, Uncle Warren; how about some tips on how to achieve your Zen-like level of financial composure?

There are two reasons why people like Buffett tell you to be patient but don't give any more instructions than that. First, Buffett's aphorisms are meant to be a great way of telling you something without really telling you anything. If the stock market is indeed a device for transferring money from the impatient to the patient, then Buffett has been on the good end of that deal for decades. You don't become the richest man in the world by giving away your true trade secrets.

But there is probably a more fundamental reason why champion long-term investors like Buffett would never bother to write this book. They have been in this game so long, as in the case of Buffett, almost seven decades, that their mental processes and techniques are now automatic. They have such a fundamental, core way of thinking about things that it rarely occurs to them that there are other ways to think. They have practiced patience for so long that they hardly even have to think about it anymore.

As we discussed before, your mind comes from your brain and your brain is part of your body. And bodies can be trained.

One person who trained both his body and mind to a state of near perfection was Michael Jordan. What Warren Buffett is to investing, Jordan is to basketball. Of course, Jordan was born with a freakish amount of raw talent. But so are most NBA players. What really set Michael Jordan apart was his maniacal training regime:

'To his teammates and coaches, he was notorious for his diligent work ethic. Jordan's longtime coach, Phil Jackson, once wrote that Michael "takes nothing about his game for granted."

He spent so much time preparing for competition that when it was game-time, he didn't have to think about what to do next'. (November 30, 2016, Willa Rubin)

If you had asked Jordan, very specifically, how to win an NBA game, you might have been given some general tidbits of advice. But mostly, he had practiced his moves so many times that it all just happened. Think of the emotion and psychological shock of playing in front of tens of thousands of screaming fans and knowing that millions more are watching you at home! Jordan practiced and practiced until there was no emotion or shock that could throw him off his game. He internalized his game until he became one of the greatest athletes of all time.

I would like to turn you into the Michael Jordan of investing. But that would be a big promise. What I can promise you is that the rest of this book will focus on the mental tools and tactics that will help you keep your calm, even when the markets are not going the way you would like. Just like the Marshmallow Children or Michael Jordan, you will have a list of specific exercises that will keep you from losing your cool and making unnecessary and unwise moves in the market. Jordan would surely tell you that champions are not born; champions are made. I intend to teach you how to bring your 'A' game to the market for the rest of your life.

Chapter 2: Don't Buy Stocks, Buy Businesses

Perhaps the most fundamental, easy way for you to change your behavior around your stock market investments is simply to re-define what a stock is. Actually, I wouldn't say 'redefine' is an accurate description. What you are trying to do is simply define accurately something that becomes distorted in a lot of people's minds.

At its most basic level, one share in a publicly-traded business means that you own a percentage of that business. This would be no different at all than if you owned one third of a family dry cleaning business. The only real difference is that in a publicly traded company, the ownership units are more easily bought and sold to strangers without permission from the other partners. This is what we call liquidity: the ability to easily buy and sell. So, the only real difference between owning one third of a family dry cleaning business and 0.003% of General Electric (GE) is that the ownership of General Electric is easier to buy and sell (it is more liquid). This liquidity should be a really good thing as it just makes life easier for the company's owners. However, too many people turn what should be an asset into a liability. Just because you can buy and sell your GE stock with ease, that doesn't mean you should!

This mental separation between direct ownership of a small business and indirect ownership of a large business is where people get lost. In fact, there is a whole industry built around mentally divorcing those two things. People who treat stock shares as units of ownership in a business are called investors. People who treat stock shares as widgets to be bought, sold, borrowed, or optioned are traders.

As we discussed earlier, traders rarely make money in the long haul. There are all kinds of psychological reasons why people get sucked into trading instead of investing.

There are three kinds of traders, and you should be none of these. The first kind of trader operates in a realm where stock shares and share prices have been completely divorced from the underlying fundamentals for the individual company or even the broader economy. They have developed a deep voodoo science, where they divine, by signs and portents, the direction of share prices by the day, by the hour, or even by the minute! They have all kinds of mystical techniques that have to do with numerical patterns, the way a pattern looks on a chart, or even mumbo jumbo that is spit out by software. They have their own specialized vocabulary that has nothing to do with the fundamental long-term earnings of the companies that they own.

The second kind of trader doesn't necessarily want to be a trader, they just feel like they know better than anyone else. They follow every news break about a company, they scour every report, they follow all of the commentators on the internet. They 'know' when things are headed in the right or wrong direction and they act accordingly. They are a firm and confident hand behind the wheel and they know best. In these cases, these traders are typically over-confident, less well informed than they think, and poorly employing their precious time.

The third and last kind of trader is actually the opposite of the character we just discussed. Rather than over-confident, they are under-confident. They also follow every news break, scour every report, and all of the commentators on the internet. But, in their case, their constant buying and selling of stocks is based on fear. They are constantly worried about their shares losing value, they don't view any dips as temporary, and they feel they need constant vigilance to avoid disaster in an inherently risky market.

Trading Debunked, Again

I won't even bother to spend a lot of time disparaging the first kind of trader. This is the day trader; the 'technical analyst; the person who has three screens on their desk and believes in things like 'levels of support', 'candle patterns', and 'breakouts'. As discussed earlier, every study in the world demonstrates that few people make money this way consistently over time. At any rate, the world of the technical trader is a totally different realm and not actually the most common form of trading.

The second two types of trader, the overconfident trader and the underconfident trader, are much more common because they are driven by two things: uncontrolled emotion and poor fundamental understanding of how Corporate America works.

The overconfident trader essentially takes an inherently passive investment and tries to turn it into an active investment. This makes no sense if you understand how truly wealthy people operate.

It may seem cruel, unfair, or just plain mean, but the reality is that truly wealthy people don't work much. In fact, everyone else works for them. A great example of this is Michael Bloomberg, the erstwhile presidential candidate, three term mayor of New York City, and legendary entrepreneur.

Bloomberg is one of the richest men in the world. His mind-boggling fortune is larger than the total net worth of many sovereign nations. How on earth did he achieve this? Bloomberg invented a machine called the "Bloomberg Terminal", which is used by security investors and analysts all over the world. Almost every stock broker in almost every country has at least one of these very expensive machines.

To this very day, Bloomberg owns 85% of Bloomberg, LP. The firm is classified as 'private', meaning that the people who own the other 15% can't just willy nilly sell shares on the open market.

You would think that owning such a huge company with billions of dollars in revenue and products all over the world would be a lot of hard work. It is, for someone. Just not the owner, Michael Bloomberg. He hasn't run his own company for 20 years.

While owning 85% of his eponymous business, he also ran the largest city in America for 12 years. Do you think the Mayor of New York City has a lot of time for other side gigs? At some point, Bloomberg hired staff to run Bloomberg LP and the beast of a company proceeded to run itself. This left Bloomberg ample time to run New York City and attempt to run for president, or anything else he might choose to do. But what he doesn't spend time on is running the company that he owns.

What is the point of all this? The point is, the real money is never in working. The real money is in owning. Whether you own 85% of a private company or 0.085% of a public company, the long-term financial gains arc merely in the ownership. Other people run the company for you so that you don't have to. The overconfident investor thinks he is adding value by constantly second-guessing the management team that he employs.

Is the overconfident investor likely to add value by reading up on the company's every gyration and then making his own moves?

The answer is 'no', for two reasons. First, empirically, we have already gone over the wealth of data that shows that the more investors trade, the more they lose in the long run. The overconfident investor is also likely to destroy value for several intrinsic, logical reasons.

All kinds of media coverage is constantly devoted to the large, often mind-boggling, pay packages that top executives can earn in Corporate America. Whether or not these pay packages are excessive is always a matter of debate. However, there is one thing that I can assure you. $20,0000,000 or more in annual compensation often hires you one hell of a good manager.

I say 'often' and not 'always' because anyone who has been investing long enough can identify one or two stories of abusive or incompetent CEOs who slithered their way into the boardroom of some major American Corporation. But, generally, you get what you pay for. C-Suite executives in Corporate America have typically beaten thousands of other candidates for that top job and they generally work much harder than you and know a lot more about that specific business. They also tend to be absolutely ruthless.

I once had a friend who graduated from the Ivy League and promptly landed a job at one of the top law firms in the world. He began to specialize in corporate law. In addition to the massive paydays and cutthroat culture of his own law firm, he also wound up with an unusual window into the C-Suites of some of America's largest publicly traded companies.

Sounds like a great gig, right? Not really. In fact, it was a nightmare. It was as close to modern slavery as is still legal. He worked 12 hours a day for six (and sometimes seven) days a week. He was expected to work holidays and nights and often, literally, slept in the office. Do you know why he was expected to work so hard at his law firm?

Because his corporate clients were working those very same hours. Week after week, month after month, year after year. His insight? The big pay package isn't just to motivate the CEO at the top of the corporate pyramid, it's to motivate the hundreds of underlings who dream of one day bringing home The Big Paycheck. Every one of these corporate slaves works grueling hours without compromise to make the share price rise. The very same shares that you own. In short, when you own shares in Corporate America, you have thousands of people doing the work so that you don't have to.

Leaving aside the inhuman hours that top corporate executives put in on your behalf, there is also the simple question of expertise. I would never advise anyone to own less than 10 stocks. I would always advise an investor to be somewhat knowledgeable about the companies that they own. But no one is an expert in all things. In a 10-stock portfolio, one might own shares in a computer company, a car company, and pharmaceutical firm. The overconfident investor somehow imagines that they are an expert in all of these different fields. Unlikely. Each company is paying big money to hire the best and brightest in each specialized field. They have toiled years in a specific field to gain specific knowledge that you just aren't going to acquire by staring at your computer screen for hours on end.

Lastly, those very well-paid experts that you employ as corporate shareholders are often ruthless when it comes to creating shareholder value. It is well documented that these corporate managers will do almost anything (and sometimes, anything) to make that share price go up. Of course, this is a double-edged sword. Sometimes, aggressive and assertive can become criminal.

As a shareholder, you wouldn't want criminality. But there are plenty of other perfectly legal but terribly unpleasant things your executives do on your behalf so you don't have to. While you are out playing golf or going to the beach, they are busy firing underperforming employees or outsourcing jobs to Myanmar. Not fun, but profitable. You are already paying someone else to do the dirty work for you. Why make more work for yourself by constantly trading?

In short, the overconfident trader believes they are adding value when they're not. They are trying to take something that is inherently passive, and trying to turn it into a job. If you're bored, get a new hobby. It's likely to cost you a lot less than constantly trading stocks.

What about the under-confident investor? They suffer from a lot of the same delusions as the overconfident investor. The under-confident investors think that they know better than the highly-paid experts that they have already hired to run their company. In this case, they're not driven by arrogance or boredom, but by fear. Stocks go down as well as up, and if they're not watched carefully, the under-confident investor fears that they could lose everything.

Of course, it's unlikely that, if you have already hired expert race car drivers, your car is going to crash. But it's also simply not factual on a mathematical basis.

Simply put, large, profitable publicly-traded companies have a strong tendency to stay large and profitable for long periods of time. Once a company is listed on the S&P 500 (the largest 500 companies in the United States), it tends to stay on that list for at least 20 years (see innosight.com). If you had bought a simple index fund of those same large stocks, you would have averaged a 10.5% annual return over the last century (see investopedia.com).

There would have been a few scary years along the way, but all in all, that broad index has only declined more than 10% four times since 1960. Remember our Rumpelstiltskin example and his $1 that compounded over time? That example factored in those occasional very bad years. The fearful investor has nothing to fear as long as they are diversified and long-term.

Gas Station or Exxon Mobil, whatever...

Perhaps you recognize yourself as one of the over-eager traders described above? That's ok, everybody is human. The mental tactics that I am about to discuss will immediately help you improve your performance and claw back your precious free time.

If you suspect that you may be the over-confident trader, just remember: You are already paying big bucks to highly experienced and skilled management to manage your investment for you. Most extra management would be a waste of your time.

Let's go back to the family business analogy. This time, let's say it's a gas station instead of dry cleaners. You own one third of a highly-profitable station, along with your other siblings. Your family has hired someone else to manage the station for you. Why? Because it's a grind and because the management may not even matter that much. If it's a good location with a nice looking store, you will sell a lot of gas. You just need someone reliable to show up every day, turn on the lights, and manage the day-to-day details. You don't want to do it yourself because you have better things to do with your life and reasonably competent management can be hired at a price that makes sense. This is how most successful businesses run.

Owning shares in a gas company like Exxon Mobil is no different. You own a smaller share in the company, but the actual dynamic is no different. If the world needs gas and there are only so many super major companies that can produce oil, you are going to sell a lot of oil and make a lot of money. If the world experiences an oil crash, then you are going to make less money. Skilled management can make a difference on the margins. But really, it's no different than the small gas station. Running that business day-to-day is one hell of a grind, so just pay someone else to do it and go to the beach.

I find it helpful to research the background of the management team I hire. Of course, the best time to do this is before you purchase shares. Since we are talking about public companies, the information about them is all over the web. You can find the biographies of the top few executives (the 'C-Suite') directly on a company's website, on LinkedIn, or through interviews in the Media. Chances are, you will be impressed by a laundry list of world-class executive positions that they have held and a strong track record of success. If you add up the industry experience of the top three or four executives in the company, they often have more than a century of experience in the kind of business that they are managing. Do they really need another manager? (You?) Are you really going to add value as the computer cowboy? Obsessing over details found through your personal computer doesn't rationally hold a candle to your management team's decade of hard-earned experience.

The next time you get an itchy computer finger while going through your online brokerage, just envision that gas station. Would you really want to spend your time managing something dirty and dull? Why would you waste your time when you've already hired someone to do that boring work? Turn off your computer and go to the pool. Enjoy. Your investment performance is someone else's responsibility. If they don't meet some pretty high standards over time, you can bet they will be fired. You have better things to spend your time on.

But perhaps you are not the overconfident investor? Perhaps you are constantly making portfolio changes due to fear? Yes, you have hired good people to run the corporations you own, but if they screw up, it's your hard-earned wealth that gets hurt.

If you find yourself trading through fear, I would urge you to review the data from earlier in this book. Think of our financial Rip Van Winkle! His $1 turned into $2900 while he was asleep for 75 years. He would have turned $100,0000 into $2,900,000 while never selling a single stock. Are you really going to do better than that through your constant buying and selling? Just like the overconfident investor, you have better things to do with your life. Turn off the computer. Go to the beach. Forget you even own the stocks.

There is one other trick I will share with you that will greatly boost your confidence. One of the cruelest facts about business is that "the rich get richer, while the poor get poorer." This is sad, but 100% true. Why is this? Simply put, it's because the Rich don't need the money, so they can ride out tough periods, and they don't get all that concerned by temporary portfolio dips. Why would they? If your assets greatly exceed your liabilities, it's not going to make a practical difference if your portfolio has a bad year, or even a couple of bad years. This feeling of security helps rich investors stay calm, cool, and collected. Not only do they not sell in down markets, they may actually buy.

What if I told you that you don't even have to be rich to use the same tactics? In the next chapter, I will teach you how to banish fear-based trading through proper asset allocation. It's easier than you think.

Chapter 3: Building A Solid Base

Imagine that you are going to custom-build your dream home. You have spent hours on end with architects and contractors planning all of the parts of the house that will give you pleasure over the coming decades. Your living room has been arranged and rearranged until you know it's just right. Your kitchen will have all of the finest appliances and be ready to host many joyful family meals. Your master bedroom will be a sanctuary for you and your significant other, and you are dreaming of lounging in there for many satisfied years.

What you probably aren't spending a lot of time fantasizing about is your foundation. You know, the solid base that nobody sees, but keeps the house safe and intact. The unglamorous concrete blocks that help your home resist storms, earthquakes, and the simple passage of time.

We never snap on HD TV and see a couple touring their potential dream home and marveling at the solid foundation that the house is built on. We should. Without that solid foundation, all the marble, crystal, and teak wood could wash away in the blink of an eye.

When we are talking about your financial home, a strong cash supply is your base. Strong access to cash in a pinch is the foundation that you will eventually build your stock holdings on. Without ample access to emergency cash, you are just building a house of cards that can blow down the next time the wind blows.

Before you buy a single share of stock, you should have at least 6 months of reserved cash stashed away in case of emergency. Your cash and credit together should equal at least 1 year of living expenses, if not more. This way, the stock market can soar, crash, and soar again without you ever needing to sell 1 share. Staying power is the number one super power for stock investors. If you want staying power, you've got to build a strong financial foundation first.

The Facts of Life

Of course, it has been very well reported over the last decade that the Rich are getting richer and the Poor are getting poorer. I don't dispute that finding; I am just going to help you be in the richer group instead of the poorer group.

Why do the rich get richer while the poor get poorer? There are a lot of reasons for this and thousands of books have been written on the topic. But the most relevant reason for this chapter is the following: rich people have better staying power and thus can turn crisis into opportunity. They rarely have to sell assets at depressed prices. In fact, when assets are depressed, the rich are typically buying. It's not fair. It's not nice. But it's the way our world works. If you play the game right, you can have staying power as well.

Obviously, I am a big fan of stock market investing. That's why I wrote this book. But I am not going to tell you that stocks only go up. In fact, I have survived at least three massive stock market crashes myself. Stocks sometimes go down. Temporarily.

So what's my key to survival? Whether smart or just lucky, I never needed to sell my stocks during a recession. When the market crashed, which it did, I didn't enjoy it, but I remained calm. Why? I didn't need the money. I knew I would need the money eventually, but not any time soon. That is what my emergency fund is for.

I am only human. I sometimes faced difficult decisions during moments of financial crisis, but I never needed to sell the gift that keeps on giving, which was my stock portfolio. I dipped into my emergency cash fund, I even took out some modest loans, but I left the stocks alone. I knew that if I kept them, they would eventually rebound. But if I sold, I would be cooking the goose that lays the golden egg.

Over the years, I went to some pretty extreme lengths to build up that cash reserve and avoid selling my stock shares. But it worked. I survived crash after crash because I made sure that I didn't need the money. It's cruel. It's not nice. It's downright sadistic. But it's the way the world works. Rich people make more money because they don't need money. When everyone else is selling, they are buying cheaply. They remain calm when the world is falling apart because they have enough cash reserves to ride out the crisis. You should strive to do the same if you want to successfully build wealth in the stock market over time.

How Much is Enough?

There is no one size fits all 'magic number' that represents an adequate reserve fund. But the number should equal about six months of your monthly expenses. So, let's say you spend about $5000 per month on rent, food, transport, etc. You should have about $30,000 sitting in a savings account before you buy one share of stock. If you spent about $3000 a month, you would need $18,000 in a savings account before you can really start investing.

Does that seem like a lot of money to you? If so, then do whatever you need to do to bring down your monthly expenses and up your saving rate. It is hard for most people; that is why most Americans will remain wage slaves their whole lives if they are even lucky enough to be employed their whole lives. Move in with your parents, share a house with another family, ride the bus instead of a car. Yes, all of these options suck. But living in constant fear because your bank account is anemic also sucks. More cash on hand and lower expenses means less fear. Less fear will eventually lead to more wealth. Much more wealth.

I actually don't think that 6 months of cash on hand is enough, especially if you are an entrepreneur or white-collar executive. Why? If you were to lose your job or your business (which happens, often through no fault of your own), it would take some time to replace that good job or good business; maybe a lot of time if you got laid off during a recession. You want to be able to take your time looking for new income. Again, that cash in the bank gives you power. Power to not sell your assets during a recession, power to not accept a bad job at low pay.

If you wanted greater security you could keep up to a year's worth of cash on hand. Unfortunately, with today's super low interest rates, our current economy punishes savers. Your cash savings are likely to earn very little or no interest, which actually means you'd lose money over time. So try this instead.

A Word About Credit Cards

Any financial advisor would tell you to stay away from credit cards. They charge absurd interest rates and screw you over with egregious fees that are often disguised in tricky ways. This rule of thumb is generally true. Credit card companies prey on the ignorant, uninformed, and the irresponsible.

But what if I told you that if you are in fact educated, informed, and responsible that you can prey on them?

There are a few fundamental facts about the credit card business that mean that you can dominate them if you are shrewd and responsible.

The first fact is that we don't have debtors' prisons in America. Chase Bank can call you seven times a week to bug you, they can even sue you, but they can never put you in jail for non-payment. They also can't send a crew of 300-pound thugs to your house to collect. If you are savvy about credit card debt, the truth is, you have them over a barrel. Not the other way around!

The second, more important fact, is that credit card companies vigorously compete with each other to make what they hope will be high interest rate loans to you. This competition means that you can play them off each other to get the best terms and conditions for you.

The third and last important fact is that credit card companies now compete with all kinds of non-bank lenders, which will further lower the interest rate you pay if you are responsible and savvy.

The entire credit system is built to abuse and manipulate uneducated chumps. If you have invested the money and time to read this book, then you clearly do not fit that description. You can develop a strategy to use credit as a resource, but only in times of need.

Remember why rich people get richer? Because they don't need money. Perversely, the same apples to credit cards. The time to build up your credit is when you don't need the money. If you are wise about building up your credit history when times are good, you can lean on that good history when times are bad.

For example, let's consider Steve Smith. Steve makes $8000 a month as a junior executive and has been doing well at his job throughout most of his 20s and early 30s. Steve comes from a modest financial background, but he believes in investing and has been proactive. So, Steve has saved up $36,000 in a savings account and his stock investments currently total $100,000. He has worked very hard to get to this point. Of his $8,000 income, he only spends about $6500 every month. During his mid-twenties, he endured living with his parents for a few years until he could build up some savings. He drives a lightly-used car.

Steve pays a lot of his monthly bills on his credit card, because he likes to get the points. He pays his bill off in full at the end of every month. After a few years of doing this, he starts to get offers in the mail. He ignores them for a long time, but eventually he gets a very attractive, low interest rate offer on a second credit card, so he signs up. Even though he only uses a fraction of his credit limit every month and he pays off the card in full every month, once a year or so, he calls up both card companies and asks for a raise on his credit limit. As time goes by, they ask less and less questions and they just raise his limit. Before he knows it, his two credit cards have a combined limit of $30,000.

Steven continues in his job and does well, year after year. However, eventually, the economy crashes, the stock market crashes, and sales at his company start declining rapidly. On his desk, Steve has had an offer for a third credit card that has been sitting around for months. They want to lend him $20,000 at 0% interest for 18 months. He doesn't think he needs the money, but, fearing a layoff, he takes the loan. The credit card company sends him $20,000 within days that he will not have to pay off for 18 months.

Three months later, Steve's worst fears are confirmed and he is laid off. It's nobody's fault. The economy took a dip, the company has suffered, and there isn't enough work to go around.

During the same time, Steve's stock investments have tanked. His $100,000 in stock is now worth only $70,000! He has no job, no income, and his stocks are suddenly plummeting. Should he panic? Should he sell everything quick, now, while he still can?

Nope. Steve is a cool customer. He has been preparing for this day for quite some time. He currently has $36,000 in cash savings, plus $20,000 in the 0% interest loan from the credit card company, plus $30,000 in the credit limit on his credit cards.

Steve really worked hard on that job; he gave it everything he had and it still all went wrong. That's a tough pill to swallow. So he takes a month off. He goes to the beach every day. He plays with his kids more. He paints some stuff in his house that his wife has wanted painted for a while. He knows that he spends about $6500 in a month. He calculates that he has at least a year's worth of reserves before he would even have to touch his stock. Steve is relaxing and regrouping, instead of panicking and cringing in fear, because he is ready.

The next month, he starts looking for a new job. It's not easy! The economy is bad; few are hiring. He gets a few interviews, but they go nowhere. Three months later, he gets an offer, but it's for substantially less than he used to make and he would need to commute 1 hour every day. He turns it down.

After 8 months of looking, he finally finds a new job. He has spent about $52,000. First, he spent the $20,000 no interest loan. Then he started charging on his credit card. At the end of 8 months of unemployment, Steve still has $36,000 in emergency cash and hasn't touched his $70,000 in stock. He does now have $52,000 in debt that needs to be paid off.

Steve would have a lot of options from here. If the new job goes well and he starts to feel more secure, he could pay off the high interest credit cards immediately, applying a portion of his $36,000 emergency cash to pay off that high interest debt. After that, he can make monthly payments on the no interest loan that he took. They only start charging interest after 18 months. So much of that debt can be paid off with no interest.

Two years after the incident, Steve has paid off most of his debt, he has started to rebuild his emergency fund, and the stock market has rebounded as the recession has slowly ended. His stock is now actually worth more than three years ago. Now his stock is worth $130,000. Because he never sold the stock, Steve has barely lost any money through the whole ordeal of being laid off during a recession. In fact, in just a few years, he will have made money, despite not working for 8 months.

Cash is King

Of course, there are a million different scenarios where the math would look different for all of the different people reading this book. But if there is one point to be made from the above example, it's the following: money is power. Including the power to say "no". When the market crashed and buyers would only offer bad prices for Steve's stock shares, Steve simply said, "No", because he had cash in the bank. When he went on those first few job interviews and the job offers were low, he simply said, "No." Again, because he had cash in the bank. This is why the rich get richer. If they don't get the offer they like, they just walk away. Guess what? They tend to get better offers.

You can too. This isn't a book about hoarding cash. It's a book about building wealth through the stock market. But having ample cash in the bank gives you the intestinal fortitude to say "No" to bad deals. As an owner in many lucrative corporations, you would never want to sell those shares unless you got a great offer. Even then you might not want to sell. Setting yourself up so that you don't need the money to begin with makes all the difference.

The next time a friend takes you on a tour of the dream house that they just bought and they waste time babbling on and on about the pantry, the master bath, or the pool deck, just quietly ask yourself, "What is the foundation made of? How many hurricanes has the house survived? How many earthquakes can this foundation withstand?" These are the questions that make a difference. These are the questions that will make you rich.

Chapter 4: The Serenity Of The Roller Coaster

Why on earth would anybody go on a roller coaster? Before they even get on the ride, they can plainly see that it will fly up, then down, then sideways at gut-wrenching speeds. These days, they flip upside down, inside out, and move fast enough to exert enormous pressure on the riders. Given the white-knuckle ride awaiting even the bravest person in the amusement park, why would anyone voluntarily get aboard?

Millions of people every year choose to ride roller coasters for two main reasons. Firstly, even though the ride will feel like a hurricane, they know ahead of time that the ride ends well 99.99% of the time. Secondly, they do it for the sheer thrill of a tumultuous rocket ride. Knowing ahead of time how the ride ends, the thrill seeker can just lie back and enjoy the sensory shock of all the ups and downs.

The stock market is no different. I love the stock market and I love what the stock market has done for me, but I would be lying if I told you that it has been a smooth ride. In my 20 plus years in the market, there have been some real nausea-inducing twists and turns. But I held on. Not because I am smarter or braver than anyone else. I simply knew what the end of the ride would look like. Profit. Big profit. I didn't need a crystal ball or a zealot level of faith. As we have discussed in earlier chapters, stocks have reliably made money for hundreds of years. There has been a lot of drama, a lot of ups and downs, but ultimately, just like the roller coaster, the stock market has delivered investors to a fixed destination decade after decade. That destination is profit.

The most important mental, and even emotional, lesson to learn is an exercise in vocabulary comprehension. Simply put: Volatility is not risk.

For some reason, the media tends to use these two words interchangeably, but that is an abuse of the English language. Again, think of the roller coaster. Of course, roller coasters are volatile by definition. But they aren't risky. They feel risky. That is what generates the excitement. But, ultimately, roller coasters are mostly thought to be a safe form of entertainment, which is why whole families often ride together. Kids ride roller coasters, grandmas ride roller coasters. They certainly are volatile, but they aren't dangerous, because the outcome is a lot more predictable and controlled than it appears from the outside.

You know what is actually very dangerous? Driving 2 miles down the street to your local convenience store to buy a loaf of bread. In fact, according to the Insurance Institute of Highway Safety, there were 33,654 fatal motor crashes in the United States in 2019, 70% of which occurred less than 10 miles from home! Considering this data, simply driving to your local school to pick your kids up should be an experience in terror. Unlike the roller coaster, there is, in fact, a real chance that you and your loved ones could die. Which seems scarier? Driving at a reasonable speed in good weather to your local Target to do some shopping or strapping into one of those massive roller coasters that makes you nauseous with fear before the ride even starts?

The point of this thought experiment is to demonstrate human fear and that the reactions to that fear are often not rational. Fear may not be data-based. It's just based on feelings. Your feelings tell you that a rollercoaster is dangerous, but driving a mile to pick up some milk feels safe. The cold hard facts would tell you the exact opposite.

It's just the same with investing. While stock markets are certainly volatile, study after study shows that, over time, they deliver reliable profit to those who are calm and patient. The fact that share prices go up and down has nothing to do with the end destination.

You might recall, every once in a while, reading some article about a freakish tragedy that occurred on a rollercoaster. In these rare cases, what typically goes wrong is that the rider exits the vehicle when they shouldn't. Something is wrong with their restraints and they go flying out of the roller coaster. Personally, I have never read about a roller coaster crashing. I have read the occasional article about someone slipping out of their seat.

It's the same with the stock market! If you just stay put, through ups and downs, twists and turns, you will arrive safe and sound at your destination. If you allow yourself to exit the coaster during one of its epic drops or twists, you'll have problems. Don't sell during the next market crash; just hold on tight and think of the drop as an inevitable and safe part of the ride. What is not safe is trying to exit the ride at the wrong time.

Chapter 5: Fear The Tax Man

S peaking of feelings that induce nausea, here is a feeling that most people hate: writing a check to the IRS. Not just paying taxes; actually sitting down and writing a check to the IRS.

What would be the difference? Well, unless you are a small business owner, you probably work somewhere for a paycheck. In that case, the process of paying the Devil his due is automated. Most workers, even highly paid executives, simply get a check twice a month, with the taxes already deducted. If they go out of their way to check their pay stub, they may not like what they see. Otherwise, the pain is automated away. That is not an accident. Both Uncle Sam and Corporate America do better when the Average Joe doesn't fully understand what is going on.

However, if you own a portfolio of growing stock, then you are no longer a worker, but an owner. As an owner, the ritual around payment of taxes is much different and, in my opinion, much more painful. There is no automating away your yearly tax payments when you are a stock investor. On a yearly basis, you must actually sit down, look over what you have made that year, and actively "Render Unto Caesar" whether by paper check or electronic payment. This is akin to a patient being fully awake during surgery without anesthesia.

Different people react differently to the unpleasant sensation of watching a large percentage of your money disappear into thin air. Some hem and haw and try cutting every corner. Others stamp their feet, curse Uncle Sam and the Stars Above, and just write the check. A few go to criminal tax avoidance lengths altogether.

Even those high net worth individuals, who believe in a more socialized form of society, in which the wealthy must "pay their fair share", still barely tolerate the pound of flesh that is extracted on a yearly basis. Even for the most idealistic, that yearly tax bill is kind of like eating your broccoli: necessary, salutary, but not something to look forward to. But if you want to be an owner instead of just an employee, you just have to pay the taxes on your stocks and get it over with.

Or do you? What if I told you that some of the richest people rarely pay taxes on stocks? What if I told you that the secret to keeping your taxes low had nothing to do with shady Swiss Bank Accounts or armies of accountants? If I could tell you a simple way to keep your taxes very low, wouldn't that be a better feeling than being mugged by Uncle Sam every year?

What Warren Knows

Here it is. The big secret to keeping your taxes low and feeling good about it. Don't sell. Do. Not. Sell. Your. Stocks.

As of 2020, wealth is not taxed in America. Income is taxed. So the paper value of your stock holdings can grow and grow (and grow), but until you actually sell the shares and convert them into cold, hard, cash, you pay very little tax.

Warren Buffett, perhaps the greatest investor who has ever lived, is very keenly aware of this. In fact, Buffett is famous for declaring, "I have a lower taxation rate than my secretary." In some ways, this is a gross exaggeration, but Buffett is only being blunt. Whether or not this arrangement is fair or good for society is beyond the scope of this book. But I can certainly teach you why the American tax system is good for you.

Do you need to be a Certified Public Accountant to understand why stocks can (and should) be managed in such a way as to minimize taxes? No. All you need to understand are a few basic principles.

For a variety of reasons, rank and file employees actually pay a higher tax rate than owners of assets in America. The details on this vary depending on which political party is in power at the time, but, generally, taxes on Capital Gains and Qualified Dividends are between 15% and 22%. Taxes on the income you make as an employee can range all the way up to 37% and have historically gone as high as 90%! Capital Gains are the kind of cash produced when you sell a stock for more than what you bought it for. Qualified Dividends are dividends that are paid by a publicly-traded company that you own.

It certainly feels better to pay 22% than 39%. But what if I told you that the optimal taxation rate for most stock investors is 0%?

Once again, you only pay taxes on actual cash that comes out of your companies. This is why Berkshire Hathaway, the ultra-profitable company that Warren Buffett founded, has never paid a dividend in its half century of existence. Dividends are nice, but dividends means taxes. Instead Uncle Warren takes the prodigious free cash flow that his company creates and reinvests it right back into the company. This is why, if you had been lucky enough to invest $1000 with Buffett way back in 1965, you would now be sitting on $27,000,000, all without paying a dime of tax.

Of course, you only would have realized this return if you'd held onto the shares that long. If you had sold during a stock dip or a stretch of underperformance, you would have suffered in two ways. First, you would have missed out on stock price appreciation, which never seems to end. Second, you would have paid taxes for that privilege. Warren Buffett has rarely sold. The same should be true for you.

Trading vs. Investing

What if you buy and sell a lot? What does that taxation picture look like? If you dare, imagine the proverbial "death by a thousand cuts". That is what our taxation system does to the capricious trader.

Right off the bat, the active trader pays at least 20% tax on any profits, as opposed to 15%. Uncle Sam taxes you more if you sell a stock after holding for less than a year. Ok, so it's only a 5% difference. Who cares? What difference does 5% make?

It turns out, it makes a lot of difference. In fact, the more you trade, the more you get hit with that 5%, and the more the damage is compounded. Remember the concept of compounding returns? That was how Buffett turned $1000 into $27,000,000 over 50 years. Now imagine that very same mathematical phenomenon working against you. Ouch.

In fact, Goldman Sachs has taken the time to quantify the impact of tax efficiency on overall returns. They calculate that $200,000, invested in a tax-efficient manner in the stock market, should become $1,002,000 over 25 years. The same $200,000 invested in an account with more buying and selling only grows to $600,000. So, in this example, that 5% taxation difference added up to more than $400,000 in lost earnings over time (gsam.com, "The Power of Tax Deferral").

Say goodbye to your dream retirement beach house. That went to the Feds instead.

Of course, Goldman Sachs knows a lot about money and investing, but they also know a lot about getting money from you. Investment bankers are always trying to sell something. So maybe we should look for a more objective viewpoint?

Dr Stuart Lucas and Alejandro Sanz, of the University of Chicago Booth School of Business, set out to measure exactly the costs of over-active stock management, with a special consideration towards taxes. The resulting study was published in the Journal of Wealth Management in the fall of 2016. After studying reams and reams of data from thousands of investors, the authors' conclusions were:

In the hunt for investment value added, taxable investors need to think differently. A low-cost, low-turnover, equity-oriented strategy with broad, consistent exposure to the market is the most likely to succeed over long periods. The power of this simple approach lies in the interaction of investment strategy, tax management, and long-term compounding. After taking into consideration taxes, the cost of being wrong, and loss-harvesting capabilities, active strategies must generate 160 to 380 basis points of value added per year just to break even with this approach. If you want to fight the active management battle, do so in the knowledge that the odds are stacked against you.

Basis points are fancy finance talk for percentages. So, in this case, frequent buying and selling would cost you between 1.6% and 3.8% of your total returns over a long period of time. This isn't a small leak in your ship. This is the iceberg that sank the Titanic.

Balance Your Feelings

Active traders typically lose out due to a toxic cocktail of factors; taxation playing a big role. This is where the smart investor trains herself to turn bad news into good news.

Most investor behavior is driven by visualizations, and the feelings attached to those visualizations. Remember the two reasons why people buy and sell too much: either over-confidence that they "know what they are doing" or under confidence, claiming that "they must sell to avoid losses".

If you suspect that you sell too often because you fall into the confident camp, ask yourself, "Is the high I get from selling this stock going to be better than the pain I will feel when I have to send 20% to the Government?" Visualize yourself writing that big check at the end of the year versus owing nothing because you didn't sell any stock. If you sell a certain stock that has wavered up and down a lot, you may or may not have more money on paper in 1 year. If you hold the stock, you will very likely have more money on paper in 5 years. If you sell, for sure, the Feds will be going through your pockets this year. Even 250 ago, Benjamin Franklin knew that "The only sure things in life are death and taxes."

If you suspect that you are in the under-confident camp, try this thought exercise. If you sell a certain stock in a panic, you may avoid a loss in the short-term, but you will be exacerbating your long-term loss for certain. Remember Goldman Sachs' missing $400,000? Those were mostly investors who felt they had to sell to avoid a short-term loss. They may have saved themselves a few bucks in the short-term, but Uncle Sam wound up with the dream beach house, not the nervous investor. Paying taxes sucks. So, sell less, pay less.

People really hate the feeling of missing out on stock market profit because they bought or sold at the wrong time. So they feel compelled to do something, even when all of the data proves that what they should do is nothing at all.

However, most people also have a natural aversion to paying taxes. It gives the same wave of disgust you feel when a cockroach scuttles around your kitchen. Selling more, triggers more taxes. Harness this natural tax aversion to talk yourself out of excessive stock trading. Your portfolio will thank you for your fortitude.

Chapter 6: The Never Ending Story

It's been almost 30 years, but I can still feel the electricity flowing through my body. The pins and needles. The sheer excitement! That was the joy of stumbling upon an undervalued treasure at a comic book store or a comic convention. There it was, Spiderman #351. the debut of a certain bad guy or a special limited-edition cover art that should have been priced at $30 but instead it was marked for just $20. Even though I was only 11 years old, I knew to play it cool. I would take the book out of the bin, lay it down, and casually just pull out some other random books. I would walk around the store, check out a book over here, over there, pretending that my found treasure was nothing special; nothing special at all. Then I would bundle it with a few other run-of-the-mill books and see if I could get a little discount off the marked price. Sometimes I couldn't, but sometimes I could! It wasn't unusual for me to pay only $15 for a book that was listed as worth $30 in valuations that used to be published monthly.

After closing the deal, like any 11-year-old customer, what would I do? Would I go home, start working the phone to my knot hole gang of fellow comic nerds, and try to immediately flip it for a cool $15 profit? Or would I hold it for a few months and then try to sell it at a comic book convention?

Hell no. First, I would take it home and carefully remove it from its protective cellophane wrapper. I'd make sure that no dogs or annoying little sisters were around who could potentially damage the prize. Then I would carefully read the comic book, pane by pane, page by page, astonished by each stroke of the pen and outlandish plot twist. If the plot was average, I would then carefully resleeve the book and place it in a special safe place in my closet to be sold "when the time was right." But if it was a really good plot, if Spiderman had saved the day using some new tactic or vanquished a particularly loathsome enemy, then the book went up on the wall of fame. I had a cork board in my room on which I would suspend my most cherished books so that I could bask in their glory at all times. I reveled in the fact that they were valuable and getting more valuable all the time (well, at least from a kid's point of view), but really, I was just in love with the stories.

What if I told you that today, 30 years later, I behave much the same way with my equity investments?

Have you ever heard the expression, "John Doe has an addictive personality"? This phrase usually has a negative connotation. For example, John finally quit cocaine abuse, but then wouldn't stop gambling at the casino. He has "an addictive personality."

It turns out that I too have an addictive personality. But I am addicted to accumulating things of value. When I was a kid, those things of value were comic books. Now that I am a grown man, those things of value are equities. And, it turns out, 'value' is not defined just as a mathematical equation (although, as we have demonstrated earlier in this book, the math certainly pencils out). 'Value' also has an emotional, sub-rational appeal. In my case, I love a good story.

It turns out that this compulsion to compile things of value runs in my family. My octogenarian uncle made an outstanding living collecting and selling medieval arms and armor. Believe it or not, he is actually world-renowned for his collection, which has been featured in the Metropolitan Museum of Art, and he has sold antique weapons to sheiks and oligarchs around the world.

When I say that he has made a very good living dealing antique arms and armor, you need to take that with a grain of salt.

I assure you that the value is real; I have witnessed him trade an ornate 17th century gun for a 6-figure check. But you didn't see the look of joy on his face that you would have anticipated. In fact, even with a 6-figure check in his hand, he seemed to be holding back a sour face as if he were sucking a lemon.

After 50 years of collecting, my uncle has the same problem that I had hoarding comic books as a kid. He loves these items and selling them feels painful. So, yes, he has built up a very significant net worth collecting antique guns. But it remains mostly a theoretical net worth, because he hates to sell.

Much like my old comic books, each antique is a finely-crafted piece of art that has a story and he will be happy to narrate the story of each piece: where it was crafted in Europe 500 years ago; the exact name and story of the craftsmen who forged the weapon; the story of the royal family who owned the weapon; even the origin of the precious metals and jewels that decorated weaponry fit for a king. Over the decades, his collecting business has become a habit so severe that he has purchased and accumulated real estate just to have secure places to store his beloved weapons. Guess what? The real estate has gone up in value as well. This is how an old crank living in rural America dies richer than many big-name corporate executives.

I'm not too different from my uncle. I have just made my life easier by accumulating things that don't have a physical presence. I have sold shares from time to time, just like I used to occasionally sell comic books and my uncle sells antiques when he must. But mostly I just freeze. Why? Each stock has a story and the story keeps me riveted. I want to see how it ends.

Once Upon A Time

The sooner you start thinking of yourself as the owner of a company and not just the owner of a simple commodity to be traded, borrowed, or bartered, the sooner you will become interested in the stories in your portfolio. And there are stories. The media never gets tired of pointing out that top corporate executives earn ungodly pay packages. But what is rarely considered is that many executives earn unusual pay packages because their lives have been journeys filled with tortuous highs and lows, devastating defeats, and, eventually, outrageous good fortune.

Whether it was Henry Ford, who went bankrupt four times before finally becoming The Henry Ford, or a book dweeb named Jeffrey Bezos, who quit Wall Street to found a little business selling books on the internet, there are some amazing tales hidden in plain sight right inside your brokerage account. Of course, more than anything, we seek value in the financial sense, but ownership in these companies also has value in the sense of the entertainment and learning that we can pick up by following the companies we own.

There are too many fascinating stories to recall in one short chapter: Steve Jobs, who was fired from his own company only to later resurrect both his own moribund company and his lagging career; Bill Gates, a social misfit who dropped out of Harvard because he thought desktop computers could change the world; of course, Elon Musk of Tesla, whose outrageous antics are also right on the border between inspirationally ambitious and just plain crazy.

Beyond mere individuals, as godlike as some of these larger-than-life executives may seem, there is also the world altering accomplishments that some of these companies have achieved. Gilead Science almost single handedly saved millions of HIV patients from sure death. The very same company cured Hepatitis C! Apple Computer put the power of the Information Age directly into your hand. As we speak, your utility companies are slowly but surely ushering in a new era of unlimited clean energy from the sun and the wind. As a shareholder, you have the power to actually participate in these stories. Every day is "choose your own adventure" when you invest in Corporate America!

The Kid Stays in the Picture

We have already established in previous chapters that selling your stocks is rarely the right move. Almost every scrap of data demonstrates that the real money is made by people who hold onto shares through thick and thin. As Warren Buffet is fond of saying, "Simple, but not easy."

Why didn't I sell my comic books even when I knew I could make a quick buck? Well, I thought they would be worth more later, but really, I just couldn't stand to part with them. Was I going to throw Captain America under the bus? Was I going to tell Batman to go fight crime somewhere else? How could I pretend that I didn't care if Wolverine died, was transported to another dimension, and was then resurrected with an all-new costume?

Leverage this story effect to strengthen your emotional resolve around your stocks. Do you really want to miss out on Elon Musk's latest antics? Gilead Pharma cured Hepatitis C. Don't you want to see what they (and you, as a shareholder) will come up with next? Ford Motor has been run by a member of the Ford family for almost a century. With all the changes coming in the automotive industry, isn't it interesting to see if a new generation of Ford motors will rise to the occasion?

This story effect is particularly powerful when the economy as a whole is in the dumps. If the market crashed by 30% in two months, don't sell! Would you walk out of the movie Superman when he is losing a fight to General Zod? Would you snap off the TV when Indiana Jones is surrounded by snakes? The most exciting part of Star Wars is when it looks like Luke Skywalker and his band of rebels are about to be extinguished. The point I want to make is: don't leave in the middle of the story!

It's the same thing with your stocks. If you build up an emotional relationship with the companies' stories and the stories of the executives who lead them, you will be less likely to bail out when the sailing gets rough. The data shows, again and again, that this reluctance to sell is a good thing.

When it comes to your own story as an investor, you are the one who gets to write that narrative. Will you be constantly buying and selling, often losing money, and wondering why you always seem to just miss the latest fad? Or will you slowly but steadily accumulate; taking joy from watching your pile grow almost as if by magic? It's up to you to decide. I can tell you that the second outcome takes a while, but eventually will feel better than you can imagine.

Chapter 7: The Way Of The Zagger

It's a sad fact that most Americans will struggle with poverty their entire lives. According to Investopedia.com, in 2017, the Government Accountability Office released a research report indicating that the average pre-retiree, aged 55–64, had just $107,000 saved for retirement. They did a lifetime of work to achieve about $6000 per year in passive income in old age.

Now, you might say that, when we use the word 'average', we are talking about folks that never went to college, folks born into poverty, folks that never did have much of a chance in life. But what about high income Americans? According to a study published by Magnify Money, using data from the Federal Reserve and the FDIC, the median high-income household has $500,000 saved for retirement. This means that even the top 10% of Americans would quickly run through savings if they were fired from their jobs or lost their health. Remember, $500,000 is the median. This means that 50% of the people who earn six figures for years, or decades, have little to show for it.

Most Americans are considered 'poor' their whole lives, and even Americans with six-figure incomes often wind up hovering around insolvency. But these must be people who foolishly spend their money on fancy vacations, flashy cars, and McMansions they can't really afford. If these high-income people invested, they would wind up rich. Not really! As we have discussed in several chapters in this book, even high-income Americans who use those high incomes to invest in the stock market tend to do badly.

The numbers are so shocking that they bear repeating. According to the DALBAR organization, a well-known financial research organization, between 1995 and 2015, the average investor underperformed the market by more than 3%. In other words, if you had simply bought a plain, vanilla index fund in 1995 and spent the next 10 years playing golf all day, you would have achieved a 7.31% annual return. But most people don't do that. They pay too much attention to their investments; buying and selling due to fear and unrestrained emotion. They only wind up with a 4.23% annual return over the very same period. However, that is the average person. In fact, many, many well paid, college-educated investors do even worse. Pitiful.

Suffice to say, the way that most people handle money is all wrong. Therefore, if you want better results than most people, all you need to do is behave differently than most people. Different behavior will bring different results. Since most peoples' financial behavior brings horrible results, you need to be different from the crowd on a regular basis to achieve good results.

You must become a Zagger...

Yields of S&P Index vs. Average Equity Investor

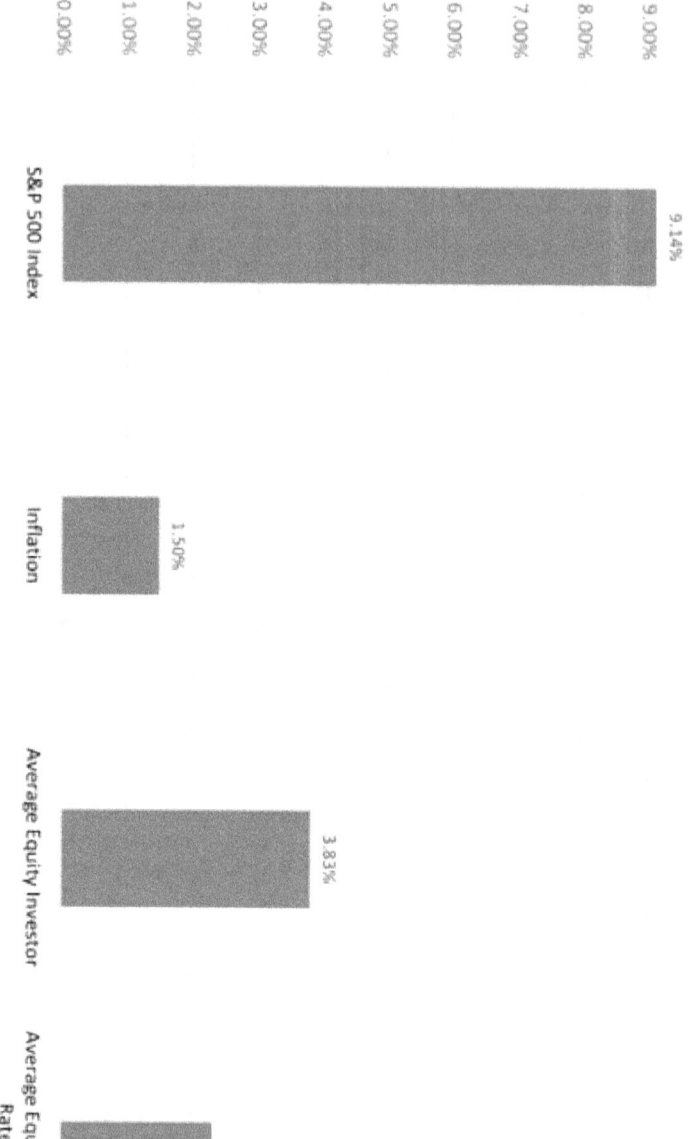

Data Provided By DALBAR Quantitative Analysis of Investor Behavior Time Period (1990-2010). Graphs & Data Analysis by Lee Rivers, Colorado College, 2020.

Zaggerism: Defined

What the heck is a 'Zagger?' Very simply, a Zagger is a person who 'zags' while everyone else is zigging. The Zagger swims upstream, even though it would be easier to go with the current. While all the lemmings gather together for perceived safety and run off a cliff, the Zagger separates himself from the crowd and runs as far away from that cliff as possible. When a house is on fire and everyone else is fleeing in a panic, the Zagger runs toward the fire because he knows that there are unguarded treasures to be plucked out of the inferno.

Zaggers are often the people who make history. Galileo Galilei was thrown in jail for daring to observe that the earth revolved around the sun. Was Galileo risking life and limb to make a statement? Was Galileo making astronomical reports just to mess with the Pope's world view? No. Galileo was simply reporting what he observed, and if his carefully measured mathematical models didn't fit with society's version of reality, so be it.

Young Bill Gates was a Zagger. While all the other kids were out playing sports or trying to impress girls with mustangs in the late 1970s, Gates was scheming about how to gain access to the world's computers, which were quite primitive at the time. He dropped out of Harvard ... Harvard! Young Bill did everything differently than most people and thus got better results.

America was founded by the greatest Zaggers the world has ever known. Throughout world history, most revolutions have been promulgated by desperate people with little to lose. The American Revolution was the exact opposite. The Founding Fathers were rich. George Washington was one of the richest men in all 13 colonies. Alexander Hamilton had overcome a lowly birth as a neglected illegitimate child to mount a promising career as a colonial official. Benjamin Franklin was not only wealthy, but a bonafide international celebrity. Sure, we see all kinds of Hollywood celebrities in the media today speaking out about pet causes and taking principled stands. But have any Hollywood celebrities been forced to tweet the following?:

"We must all hang together, or, most assuredly, we shall all hang separately."
—Benjamin Franklin.

By the way, hanging was only part of the punishment for treason against King George. George Washington, one of the richest men in the colonies, took the risk of being hung, then disemboweled, and then torn limb from limb, all because he got sick and tired of taking orders from a king that had never set foot on American soil. It really would have been a lot easier for George Washington to sit back and enjoy the life of leisure that he could afford. But at some point, he just had to do what he had to do. George Washington was a Zagger.

You know who is not a Zagger? The punk working down at your local organic brew fair trade coffee house with 20 tattoos and purple hair. That is someone small on the inside, willing to go to any lengths to get attention. Same thing for the jerk at the country club happy hour who wants to tell everyone how smart he is for playing the market with options, derivatives, and other unnecessary garbage.

The real Zagger doesn't seek attention or recognition for being different. The real Zagger often doesn't even feel any different from anyone else. They just consistently Zag while everyone else Zigs. That is just the reaction that feels normal for them.

The Original Gangster of the Zaggers

By now, you have probably noticed that I refer to Warren Buffett a lot. Warren Buffett is an icon in the investor world because he has been one of the few richest men in the world for damn near 50 years. He has also written extensively about his philosophy and personal journey, so the common man has an unusually high level of access to the mega tycoon's thought process. One of his many famous phrases is, "You must be fearful when others are greedy and greedy when others are fearful."

Warren Buffett is the original Granddaddy of the Zaggers. As of the writing of this text, Buffett is 89 years old and still highly active. From the moment we consider his career, his Zaggerism is obvious.

Think Rockefeller. What comes to mind? Oil.
Gates. What comes to mind? Computers.
Think Bezos. What comes to mind? Amazon.

Warren Buffett has been, at various times, just as rich (or richer!) than these legendary tycoons. But he is quite different. Each tycoon mentioned is associated with one big game-changing business that has generated a mind-boggling fortune. Buffett got rich by owning stuff ... lots and lots of stuff. The publicly-traded conglomerate that he controls, Berkshire Hathaway, is a random hodgepodge of assets he has acquired over the decades. If Rockefeller, Gates, and Bezos were associated with the biggest innovations of their day, Warren Buffett is the financial titan equivalent of a crotchety old grandpa who accumulates stuff that he buys cheap at garage sales. What is the saying? "One man's trash is another man's treasure." In the case of Buffett, the emphasis is on treasure.

Of course, multiple tomes have been written documenting every aspect of Buffett's astounding rise to global prominence. But the gist of his success is the following: from the late 1960s to the early 1980s, the American Stock Market vastly underperformed. Due to a variety of geopolitical factors, the market crawled along like a sickly turtle for what seemed like a very, very long time. It got so bad that no one even wanted stocks anymore. No one except Warren Buffett.

Realizing that common stocks had fallen drastically out of favor, Buffett actually found ways to use other people's money to acquire more and more shares at better and better prices. Berkshire Hathaway acquired GEICO (sound familiar?), an insurance company. He used those millions in insurance premiums to just keep piling up unloved stocks that no one else wanted.

Whether it was luck or genius, or some combination of the two, Buffett turned out to be right. Just as the 70s had been a nightmare decade for stocks, the 80s and 90s handed in year after year of scorching outperformance. By 1996, everyone and their mother was buying stocks, often at overinflated prices. It didn't matter to Buffett. He had amassed a mind-boggling stockpile of shares decades before when they were still cheap. When the world was Zigging, Warren Buffett Zagged. He behaved differently from most people, thus, he wound up with very different results. Very different results.

The Zagger is You

None of this is to say that you must risk execution by hanging (like George Washington) or control a publicly-traded international mega-conglomerate (like Buffett) to be successful. Washington and Buffett are simply famous examples that illustrate a point.

If you have sought out and paid good money for this book, you probably already have something of the Zagger in your personality. The trick is to harness that natural contrarian tendency and hone it into a razor-sharp advantage.

The most fundamental application of the Zagger mentality is to realize that stock market crashes are good, not bad. When you hear about a flash discount sale on Amazon or with your favorite retailer, do you react with dread and palpitations? No, you get excited, because a whole lot of great merchandise is about to be sold cheap for a limited time. It's just the same with stock market crashes.

Better yet, don't do anything at all! Sometimes, a Zagger can stand out from the crowd by simply not engaging in the hysteria of the masses. Go ahead, plow large amounts of money into some simple, broad index funds and spend the next 20years going to the beach and playing with your kids. The data clearly show that, while everyone else is busy running around with their hair on fire, buying, selling, shorting, and optioning, you will very likely be making more money by just doing nothing. How easy is that?

Zaggerism also helps you achieve a rich sense of humor. I view financial media, such as CNBC, as more of a comedy show than anything else. Sure, Jim Cramer and his colleagues are entertaining, but, generally speaking, they have no idea what they are talking about. We will discuss this more next chapter. It is clear that even the most grizzled Wall Street veteran or the number one graduate from Harvard Business School does not have a crystal ball to predict the future. Take a look at your friends or neighbors who breathlessly hang on the words of these charlatans and enjoy a good chuckle. As PT Barnum once said, "There is a sucker born every minute." Every two minutes, a sucker calls into "Mad Money," on CNBC.

It's common knowledge that many people take pleasure in behaving differently than others. Think about the term "sexual deviant." In a literal sense, it only means someone with a different flavor of sexuality than most people. But of course, the phrase "sexual deviant" has a bad connotation. The phrase connotes two things. First, it implies that being different is dirty, or wrong. Second, most importantly, it connotes that being different feels good.

Of course, it would be irresponsible for me to promote sexual deviance in these pages. But sex is just one way to feel good. I will wholeheartedly promote "financial deviance." Go ahead; be different, be unique, be you when you invest. You might be surprised by how good it feels.

Chapter 8: Become An Expert

Quick review question: What are the two reasons why people typically buy and sell stocks too often? Confidence. Either too much confidence or too little. The overconfident investor "knows what he is doing" and therefore believes that his constant buying and selling will add value. Of course, the data firmly indicate otherwise. The underconfident investor feels that he doesn't really understand what is going on and therefore he is exposed to a disaster that could strike at any time. He believes that his constant buying and selling is the best way to shield himself from his lack of knowledge. Again, the data prove that, typically, rather than avoiding a disaster, the buying and selling is the disaster.

The number one way to avoid either overconfidence or underconfidence is to become an expert in the companies you own. That way, when you think you know what you're doing, you actually do know what you are doing.

Warren Buffett calls this concept the "Circle of Competence". While Buffett is famous for the deals he has done and the success he has had, he is equally famous for the deals he has not done and the disasters he has avoided. He attributes a lot of success to his extreme reluctance to invest in businesses that he does not understand. Before he puts his capital (and the hard-won capital of his shareholders) at risk, he wants to make sure he understands the business. You should do the same. It's not nearly as hard as you think. In fact, you probably already understand a lot more than you think you do.

Jack of All Trades, Master of None

You may have already noticed that I have a low opinion of most financial media, especially financial 'personalities'.

Falsehood #1: 'Stock' experts know everything about every kind of stock and can be consulted, just as if you were gazing into an omniscient crystal ball.

Falsehood #2: If you don't have the same kind of expertise as these 'stock' experts, you should either not be in the game or you should be hiring and paying an expert who knows all things 'stocks'.

Above, I put the word 'stocks' into quotation marks because 'stocks' are not stocks, they are companies; little slices of companies that you own. They are no different than if you owned 100% of a local dry-cleaning chain, except, in this example, you own 0.01% of a national dry-cleaning chain with thousands of locations. When you put the investments in that context, we easily see why financial personalities are nothing more than circus performers. Who could possibly know about every kind of business around the world?

During every single show, Jim Cramer does his 'lightning round', for which people call and ask questions about their holdings in dozens of different kinds of businesses. Dozens! This would require Cramer to have expert knowledge about dozens of different kinds of business and industries. In a typical week, Cramer comments on the prospects of at least 20 different companies in 20 different industries. How could anyone be an expert in industries as diverse as defense, pharmaceuticals, software as a service, and construction?

Let's go back to the dry cleaner example. Let's say you own 100% of a small chain of local dry cleaners. Let's say you have built up ownership of 10 dry cleaners over the years. Now you have borrowed a million dollars and you want to acquire other small businesses that would be complementary to your current dry cleaning holdings. Who would be a better consultant/advisor for you? Someone who has 20 years of experience in dry cleaning/chemistry/commercial real estate or someone who barks out random predictions about 30 unrelated businesses every week?

This is why the Financial Media can provide value to equity investors, but those investors have to be choosy about who they listen to. If CNBC is running a segment about biotech companies, then they should be engaging with a noted expert on biotech companies. Likewise, if they're running a special on agriculture investments, then they should be interviewing someone who has a lifetime of experience in the farm business. I don't want to hear someone who sells stocks for a living spewing forth diatribes about ratios, value creation, or PE multiples. Get me someone who knows about the specific type of business in question.

The Expert is You

You can do very well as a long-term shareholder even if you never watch one day of CNBC and you don't even know where Bloomberg TV is on your cable package. You already know a lot more about business than you think.

There are generally two ways somebody becomes an industry expert; both are perfectly viable and worthy. Firstly, consider the knowledge you acquire over the years by working for a paycheck. In my particular case, I have been a champion salesman in the medical field for almost 20 years. Pharmaceuticals, pathology services, medical devices; I have sold it all. I have spent thousands of hours in doctors' offices, hospitals, and outpatient clinics. I have seen things from the point of view of the doctor, the medicine maker, and the hospital owner. For me, focusing on biotech and medical devices makes sense. The healthcare world is my automatic 'circle of competence'. This was why I started www.sickeconomics.com and published my first book, *Your First Biotech Million.* I had already earned the knowledge through decades of work; I just chose to lever that knowledge to achieve maximum value for myself, and my readers.

You're probably no different. Whether you are an architect, advertising salesperson, or attorney, there is probably a constellation of publicly-traded businesses that you already know a lot about. If you concentrate your equity holdings in these names, you will be a lot more competent and less likely to suffer from overconfidence or underconfidence.

Secondly, another way to become an expert in a sector is with pure passion. Let's say you're a dentist. You trained hard to become a dentist and, month after month, you make a nice, steady living this way. There's nothing at all wrong with your solid career. But drilling cavities and extracting molars has never been what really gets your heart pumping. What really makes your blood rush is the roar of a brand new Mustang or the brand new leather smell of a Porsche. You love cars. Ever since you were a kid, you dreamed of sports cars, trucks, limos... basically anything with wheels attracted your attention like a magnet. You read all of the relevant industry blogs and subscribe to some newsletters. You would do it all for free; the thrill of the open road is that powerful to you.

In this example, you would probably already know a lot about companies such as Ford, BMW, or Fiat. You probably also know the names of more obscure players, like companies that manufacture car parts. In this example, you could probably be a very successful investor in equities related to the automotive industry. Your years of research will help you make wise, patient choices related to your holdings; you're unlikely to be rattled by bumps in the road, because you know the players and you understand the evolving economics of that particular industry. In this example, who would be more fit to comment on automotive businesses? An 'expert', who just looked at his computer screen for ten minutes or you, who have followed every new car release over the last ten years?

Holding onto your shares for the long term requires a level of emotional comfort. You need to feel comfortable in the story, mission, and management of each of the companies you own. It is a lot easier to achieve this Zen-like state if you know the industry. Pick a few industries that appeal to you. Get good at understanding them.

Chapter 9: Get Busy! The Other Compounding

As we have discussed throughout this book, the data show again and again that you are very unlikely to add value to your stock portfolio through constant buying, selling, and other manipulations. Stock investments were simply built to be passive investments. Your Board of Directors and CEO already oversee the company that you own. Adding an additional layer of oversight is just like trying to drive a car while you are upside down. Sure, if you really want to, you can push the gas and brake pedals with your hands and steer the wheel with your feet, but the machine wasn't built to be used that way. You can pervert the manufacturer's design intention, but it's highly likely that you won't like the results. Your stocks drive themselves; for goodness sake, leave them alone!

But, of course, this is easier said than done. Those two psychological factors, overconfidence and underconfidence, are powerful forces that compel otherwise sound decision makers to errors in judgement. How do you block out those compulsions that creep up on so many otherwise rational people? Simple: fill up your time with other productive endeavors. The less spare time you have, the less time you have to wander around your stock portfolio looking for things to mess up.

We have already examined in detail how a little extra activity in your stock portfolio can sabotage your returns over the long term. Now let's consider how a little extra activity in the real world can turbo charge your stock returns over time. Let's look at the facts; then you can decide how best to invest your precious time.

Meet Mr. Average Joe

For the sake of this example, I am going to assume that our Average Joe is like most middle class or upper-middle class people in America. We will say that his earnings (or the earnings of himself and his spouse) are just enough to cover monthly expenses and even save a little. We'll assume that his primary money-making occupation takes up about 9 hours a day of his time.

Let's say our Average Joe earns about $90,000 a year at a job. After taxes and expenses, he manages to pay his monthly bills and save about $5,000 a year.

He's about 40 years old, and he's been diligently saving for 20 years, so between savings and compounded investment returns, he currently has a $200,000 nest egg. Not bad at all for an Average Joe!

THE THREE JOES			
	Below Average Joe	Average Joe	Better Than Average Joe
Monthly Contribution	$420	$420	$1170
Compounded Avg. Return	3%	6%	9%
Time	25years	25years	25years
Nest Egg, Age 65	$605,023	$1,185,000	$3,200,000
Data Calculated on BankRate.com			

Joe likes to get about 8 hours of sleep a night, which leaves him with 16 waking hours per day. Joe labors for a paycheck about 9 hours a day, which leaves him with about 7 hours of free time per day. He's married with two kids, so his domestic responsibilities eat up a lot of that free time. After all is said and done, Joe has about 3 hours of 'me time' per day. He rarely has to work for his company on weekends. So Joe may have up to 10 hours of 'me time' during the weekend. This 'me time' is the danger zone for a stock portfolio.

If you are truly the Average Joe, you may get bored or anxious during your 'me time', which would lead you to crack open the stock portfolio and begin the process of screwing yourself out of large profits. But, in our example, our Average Joe is just a bit better than average.

Joe Gets Busy

Instead of fooling around with his stock portfolio, he sells affordable antiques online. On weekends, he prowls garage sales and estate sales, looking for things of value that people have forgotten about. He reads the obituaries and calls up families when he knows that Grandma has passed on. After a few years of this, he actually gets to be known around town and sometimes people call him, looking to sell items they no longer want.

The extra money Joe makes this way is a nice bonus, but he mostly does it as a hobby. He likes antiques, he likes the stories behind the objects he finds, and, mostly, he loves the rush of stealing a good deal. He makes about $1000 a month this way.

A lot of people would take that $1000 and spend it on vacations, a fancy car lease, or home renovation. Not our Average Joe. He spends $250 monthly buying something extra for his kids or wife and the other $750 goes right into his stock portfolio.

Ok, so what? A lousy $750 per month into his stocks is never going to transform our Average Joe into 'More Wealthy than Average Joe', right? Well, let's see. We will use Nerdwallet.com to crunch some numbers.

Prior to Joe getting his side gig going, his family was saving about $420 per month. Let's just assume for a moment that he never did get a side gig. At age 40, he already had $200,000. So, if he attained a 6% annual return on his stock portfolio and his new monthly investments, by age 65, Average Joe would be looking at $1,185,000. Not bad at all, but not enough to afford a dream retirement.

But, starting at age 40, Joe is now going to invest $1170 per month, which is the sum of his previous $420 plus the $750 from his side gig. You'll also remember that, statistically speaking, the average 'active' investor underperforms the market by 3% every year. Between his regular job, his side gig, and his family, our Joe simply hasn't had time to obsess over his stock portfolio. The man is busy; as he acquires more and more stock, it just sits there and does its own thing, the way it was designed to do. Instead of earning a 6% annual return, Joe achieves a 9% annual return, which has been the average return of the market for many decades. In this scenario, Joe sails into age 65 with a whopping $3,200,000 in his stock portfolio!

How could there be such a huge difference in these two scenarios? How could Joe's little side gig make such a difference over time? One word: compounding.

It turns out there is a reason why Albert Einstein called compounding, "The 8th wonder of the world." Very simply, when compounding works in your favor, it's an incredibly powerful tailwind. When compounding is working against you, it's like trying to run a marathon wearing sneakers made of lead.

In our example above, Joe's little side gig actually delivers the power of double compounding. By being so busy that he has little free time left, he is likely to realize the full value of the market, which is about 9% annually. If he had time to mess around with his stock portfolio in a sad attempt to imitate Gordon Gekko, he would most likely achieve a lower return over time.

Secondly, Joe's little side income has added up over time. Joe is working hard, but Joe is also working smart. He does enjoy some of his extra income every month in the form of fancy meals out or baseball tickets. But most of it just goes into growing his net worth, month after month, year after year. The result? Some real gold in his Golden Years.

The important principle here is twofold. First, "idle hands are the Devil's workshop," as the saying goes. Too much spare time leads the mind to wander, which often leads to a stock trading habit that will cost you more than a cocaine addiction over time. Secondly, extra income steered into your investment accounts grows like wildfire over time. In our example, Joe built a side gig selling antiques online. How he attained the income is irrelevant. You could work part time somewhere; you could paint houses or work as a handyman. Just do what you must to make sure your income exceeds your monthly expenses by a wide margin and you too can wind up rich.

Harnessing the full power of compounding is certainly not as sexy as founding Tesla or writing a best-selling novel. But the simple arithmetic will get you where you want to go. The question is: How badly do you want to get there? If you want to be rich, it will require a little discipline and a lot of hard work.

Chapter 10: Birds Of A Feather

The net lesson of the last chapter was that small changes in behavior can make huge differences over time. Our Average Joe was just a little more disciplined than average, just a little more hard working, and displayed just a little more initiative. Yet he wound up with a net worth over $3,000,000; a number that will remain just a fantasy for 95% of Americans.

Maintaining that kind of financial discipline over time is not as easy as it seems, but I can tell you the easiest way right now; avoid bad influences, by which I mean certain people. Many perfectly good people are bad influences. They may be perfectly nice, ethical, decent people, but more than likely, they know nothing at all about the accumulation of wealth. These are good people with bad ideas about money. Avoid them and you've already taken the first step towards retiring with $3,000,000 while most Americans struggle to make ends meet well into old age.

To be clear, I am not advising you to suddenly cut off all contact with friends and family who are unwise about money. Simply take what they say with a grain of salt and make a concerted effort to surround yourself with people who think the way you do.

Let's return to the case of our not-so-Average Joe. Over Joe's lifetime trek to wealth, who did he likely avoid and who did he likely embrace?

Well, first and foremost, he tuned out all of the people who told him he didn't need a side gig because stock trading should be his side gig. If Joe told anyone that he had a substantial stock portfolio (he may very well have just kept that information to himself), I can guarantee that dozens of people over the years either gave or requested advice on what to buy or sell. Joe may well have engaged in some entertaining discussions about the long-term trends that he likes or a few particular companies in his portfolio that he cherishes. But he certainly avoided talking about chart patterns, short selling, trading options, buying on margin, and all of the other nonsense habits that destroy value for the 'suburban day trader' set.

Joe also very likely avoided people who insisted that he needed a new luxury car or a brand new kitchen every 5 years, or even those who insisted that his kids needed to go to an out-of-state private college. Not only did Joe show tremendous initiative and gumption in mounting a side gig, he invested the extra money instead of spending it. He may have had iron discipline, but investing instead of frivolous spending is a lot easier when your friends don't drive Mercedes and a week of camping is considered to be just as much fun as flying the family to Paris. If most of your friends are on the thrifty side, then there is no consumption pressure to begin with.

Who would Joe have embraced? Well, he probably would have a lot of fun socializing with other antique collectors and dealers. After all, it was mostly his passion for antiques that drove him to work nights and weekends; the money was just a bonus. Assuming that Joe mostly dealt in items that fit his price range ($100-$1000 dollars), he would most likely have come into contact with antique traders in the same financial range. They, in turn, would be likely to have personal finances akin to Joe's family. Thus, Joe would naturally be socializing with people whose habits he could afford.

Another place where Joe could have found companionship with like-minded individuals would be online. If you go to a smattering of real-world social events and the topic turns to investing or share purchases, you remain a victim of chance. You could find yourself amongst shrewd, disciplined investors, such as yourself, or you could be forced to listen to your 19-year-old nephew boasting about his big financial adventures on the Robin Hood trading app. If you don't control your environment, you may wind up having to filter out a lot of world views and opinions that don't fit your financial worldview.

Online, there are hundreds, if not thousands, of financial clubs and conversation groups that are divided by investing style, age group, or even industry (biotech clubs, real estate clubs, etc). If Joe chose to join an online investing community, this would give him the power to control the environment he enters. By choosing a group of conservative value investors, he has automatically screened out 90% of the absurd opinions out there. Of course, the internet is notorious for giving soap box platforms to cranks and crooks. But Joe can simply exercise the same good judgement that he has used in his day-to-day life and screen it out with the press of a button.

How to Not Be a Jerk

Even if Joe applies all of the techniques listed above, it's still likely that he will be cornered by a lot of financial idiots over a lifetime. The stock market just has a weird mystique that attracts all kinds of people, many of whom are fools. I guarantee, they will want to push some of their foolish ideas on you.

How to gracefully handle these situations? Well, one great way is to downplay your level of expertise. Joe can present facts as ideas or theories, which makes him seem more humble. Here is a list of time-honored phrases that will help you reject idiocy with grace:

-"My understanding is ..."
-"I had read that ..."
-"I wonder if ..."
-"Is it possible that ..."
-"Some people say ..."
-"Just one man's opinion, but ..."
-"In my experience ..."

Another outstanding way to refute moronic ideas about money, without sounding preachy, is to simply attribute the ideas to other people.

"I read a book by Warren Buffett, one of the world's richest people ..."

"There is a great book by an author called Benjamin Graham ..."

"I used to have a rich aunt that used to say ..."

"My old college roommate has done great and he is always saying that ..."

By this point in the book, you know how I feel about the writings and guidance provided by Warren Buffett. His ideas have influenced me a lot. So, when some young punk wants to talk about the benefits of rapid stock trading, I hardly offer my opinion at all. I just phrase it as something that I read by a famous author. The kid can take the hint or not. But the important thing is that I am not positioning myself as some kind of superior person or investment authority. I'm merely passing on some information that was shared with me and now I'm trying to help the next guy.

Feeling Good

So why do people trade so much? Why do people buy fancy cars and shiny watches? Ultimately, logic has very little to do with these financial behaviors. People are driven by feelings, and feelings cause people to throw away the earnings of a lifetime on items that bring a momentary rush.

It's very likely that our not-so-Average Joe is wired a bit differently than most. He probably couldn't have maintained that level of initiative and discipline all those years unless he took a kind of pleasure in watching his brokerage balance go up and up. While others take pleasure in watching their shoe collection grow and grow, for whatever reason, Joe is motivated by watching his stock collection skyrocket over time.

Joe is likely to get the most pleasure out of life by hanging around people who feel the same way he does. If he finds himself amongst the BMW set, he may feel lost. While they are droning on and on about the various features of their fancy new vehicle, Joe is just daydreaming about owning stock in BMW.

The point of this chapter is not to encourage a life devoid of pleasure. The point is to help you define where you find your pleasure. If you have purchased this book and read this many pages already, it's very likely that you will take mental pleasure from knowing that you could purchase 10 BMWs. Actually purchasing one will likely disappoint you and feel like a waste.

Additionally, the point of this chapter isn't to judge people who prefer to accumulate goods rather than profits. If most people really enjoy a luxury car or a fancy house, then by all means let them find their own pleasure in life. But don't be surprised when they seem stressed out and depressed, even while tooling around in their luxury automobile. Remember that bad compounding is just as powerful as good compounding. The long-term price tag of the lux lifestyle is far more than what was written on the original invoice.

Choose your friends and acquaintances wisely, control your environment, and speak with humility when possible. Accumulating wealth through shareholdings actually gets easier when you follow those principles. Good people and good surroundings will help you build the healthy mental habits that will make you rich in money and in spirit.

Chapter 11: If You Must, Part I

Most of this book has been dedicated to exploring psychological tricks and tactics to help you avoid being a frequent, overactive investor. I do believe many of you will have good success with these tactics. If you commit to practicing these mental strategies, they will become habits, and everyone knows that habits are hard to break, for better or worse.

But there are a certain percentage of people who just can't help themselves. Some people just have to be 'in the game' and no amount of rational explanation or psychological conditioning will be able to control the urge to become an active player in what should essentially be a passive game.

If you bought this book and have read this far, you probably buy into the logic of disciplined, methodical stock market investing. But that doesn't mean you will be able to control yourself. If you suspect that you just won't be able to keep your dirty hands away from your keyboard and you could trade stocks at any moment, this chapter is for you.

Afterall, everyone is human. The following two chapters will teach you how to channel your natural human impulses into positive action. If you must treat your stock portfolio as an active affair, you still have a chance to benefit. You just have to do it right.

Cash Flow

As we have discussed throughout this book, owning a sliver of Corporate America is an astoundingly lucrative proposition. Most of America's largest corporations (and many smaller ones) produce excess cash year after year, decade after decade. One of the tasks of the managers you have hired to run your corporation is to decide what to do with the torrents of cash that gush from your remunerative business.

Typically, there are three ways to leverage excess cash flow to create even more value for shareholders.

Option #1: is via mergers and acquisitions. If you own a company that makes tires, you may choose to use excess cash flow to buy a company that manufactures tire hubs. The theory would be that combining the two businesses at the right price will result in an even more profitable entity. M&A sounds great in theory, but in reality, corporate empire builders have had a very 'hit and miss' track record over the last 50 years.

Option #2: is to simply take excess cash and buy back the company's own shares. The theory would be that, by reducing the number of 'free floating' shares on the open market, each share will be worth more. The company is leveraging excess cash to create scarcity in its own shares. This approach has become a very entrenched tradition in Corporate America, but the practice has been controversial for two reasons. First, buybacks don't always raise share prices; there has often been a gap between theory and reality. Second, a lot of critics see this practice as essentially building a bonfire fueled by excess cash. It feels like an unproductive use of capital to a lot of business professors and progressive government critics.

Option #3: is the oldest, most established method of rewarding shareholders. Simply pay a dividend. Excess cash, which is produced on a predictable and methodical basis, is paid out to shareholders just the same way. Corporations have been rewarding shareholders this way since the 1600s.

Just like any other practice that has lasted 400 years, dividends have come in and out of vogue over the years. While many investors rejoice at the feeling of cold, hard cash in their hands, the practice still has its critics. For very wealthy people (who increasingly control the bulk of shares in America), any extra income creates extra taxes. Therefore, there is a class of share owners out there who actually advocate to minimize income.

Another criticism of dividends is that any extra cash should be put towards growing revenues. If cash is paid out, it often appears that management haven't been able to think of anything better to do with it. This is why, over the last several decades, high growth companies, such as tech startups and biotechs, have tended to eschew dividends. At some point, the mathematical implications of dividends become less important than the 'signal' they send to investors. Companies that want to be considered 'young guns' don't pay dividends, because they have so much more growing to do. 'Grown up' companies with mature business tend to cultivate and grow their dividends with great care; they are looking to attract a slow but steady group of owners.

When dividends are paid out to you, typically, you would have three choices to make yourself.

Option #1: spend the dividend. You could spend the dividend on something frivolous or fun, because, hey, life is short. Or you could just live off the dividend. Millions of senior citizens around the world depend on quarterly corporate dividends to pay for food, electricity, and even rent.

Option #2: set up automatic reinvestment at your brokerage. This program is sometimes called a DRIP program; if you own stock in Coca-Cola and Coca-Cola pays you a dividend four times per year, that dividend never shows up as cash in your brokerage account. Rather, the dividend immediately goes toward buying more shares of Coca Cola. This way, you are harnessing the power of compounding automatically. You can go about your life, spending your time as you please, and one day you could come back and you own a huge chunk of Coca-Cola stock. You planted the vine long ago, and one day you came back and it had taken over the whole yard. Except now you have a vine that grows money.

Option #3: take those quarterly dividends and reinvest them yourself. In this example, you are still planting seeds that will one day lead to a verdant garden. But now you'll get to play the role of Master Gardener. Each quarter, four times per year, your dividends come in, and you'll decide where to invest the cash. Sometimes, you may put it right back into the company it came from. But you may think the cash would be better invested in another company in your portfolio. In this example, you will lovingly tend your garden quarter after quarter, year after year. One day, you will also wind up with a lush garden filled with money trees. But this is more like a manicured English Garden. Nature certainly did its work, but this time she did it in partnership with a horticulturist.

If you absolutely, positively must take an active hand in your stock portfolio, the reinvestment of dividends, patiently and with discipline, is a great way to leave your mark on your money garden.

The Power of Dividends

We rarely hear about dividends in the media. Right now, we are going through a phase in which dividends are not seen as sexy, cool, or even very lucrative. In the era of the Robin Hood speculator, everybody is about quick trading profits based on price appreciation. The underlying fundamentals of a company barely seem to matter to millions of 'momentum' traders. A momentum is someone who buys the most popular stocks of the moment, betting that "momentum" will push prices from high to even higher.

However, for our patient financial gardener, cash flow matters over time. It really matters. Again, this isn't my opinion; this is the data speaking. Dr. Ian Mortimer and Matthew Page, CFA, published a study on this topic. They asked the question, "What percentage of total returns over time are related to the compounding of dividends?" The findings were shocking:

For an average holding period of 1 year, dividends accounted for 27% of total returns of the S&P 500 since 1940. If we increase the holding period to 3 years, dividends account for 38%, 5 years it increases to 42%, over a 10-year period it rises to 48%, and with a 20-year holding period, dividends account for some 60% of total returns. It is important to note, too, that here we are not just looking at the S&P 500 as a whole and not focusing purely on companies that actually pay a dividend. If we did, we think these results would likely be even more striking. (Why Dividends Matter; GAFunds.com)

Dividends matter. A lot. You may remember the three options we discussed for the investor who receives a dividend deposit. One option was to simply spend the dividend. After all, all we hear about in the media is share price. Did it go up? Did it go down? What has the share price done over the last month, the last year? You might think you could just spend the dividend with minimal consequence. Mortimer and Page did some research on that idea, as well.

DIVIDENDS MATTER					
Holding Period	1 Year	3 Years	5 Years	10 Years	20 Years
% of Total Return attributable to compounding of dividends	27%	38%	42%	48%	60%

Research by Dr. Ian Mortimer & Matthew Page
Why Dividends Matter
GAFunds.com

If you had invested $100 at the end of 1940, this would have been worth $174,000 at the end of 2011 if you had reinvested the dividends, versus $12,000 if dividends were not included.

Of course, turning $100 into $12,000 is a neat trick, but you would wind up leaving some $160,000 on the table by ignoring the importance of the dividend compounding effect.

If dividends and dividend compounding is so important, why don't we hear about the phenomenon more? Instead, we only hear "What went up today?"; "Which sector is hot right now?"

Plainly put, people are impatient and lack vision. They want profit now. Sitting around and watching a garden grow is not very sexy.

But it is sexy to the horticulturist. Millions of people across the United States pay great money towards the hobby of making things grow and making things grow the way they want. If you choose to reinvest your own dividends, you are no different.

Where is the pleasure for a horticulturist? Do they have some kind of magic button they can push to make shrubs and vines grow more quickly? Nope.

They take pleasure in knowing that their actions today will lead to greater results tomorrow. The pleasure is actually three-fold.

The first, mental pleasure, comes from building the vision. Remember, most champion gardens begin with a vision in mind: they want a proper English Garden with stiff rows of hedges that stand like soldiers; they want a tropical garden that looks like a permanent Hawaiian vacation. There is a certain pleasure in envisioning the goal.

The second mental pleasure is the physical act of working the soil. Some people use gardening as a light form of exercise or even a way to tan. Plus, sticking your hands in the dirt has certain primal appeal for a lot of people.

The greatest pleasure is watching your vision slowly become a reality. Yes, after planning and planting, the waiting is tough. But it isn't long before tender sprouts start to take root and the gardener can see green shoots arising. Bit by bit, these green shoots grow, and eventually, our patient gardener arrives at the big payoff: his vision has become reality. He has harnessed the power of nature to realize his vision.

Leveraging the power of dividend compounding is just like gardening, in that both photosynthesis and exponential compounding are forces of nature that were discovered by man, but not invented by man. That is why Albert Einstein called compounding, "The 8th wonder of the world". Compounding is a natural law that mankind discovered, and the exponential math works in all kinds of scientific and business disciplines. As the patient dividend gardener, you are planning and executing a vision to make sure that this natural law works for you.

Christmas in July

Why do holidays exist? If you love someone, why wait for their birthday to buy them a gift? Why wait for the pageantry of Christmas when you could just order something from Amazon today?

Holidays exist for two reasons. First, to enforce a kind of discipline. You may love someone, but if you buy them gifts all the time, you may well wind up broke. If you only buy during designated times that are commonly accepted throughout society, you have a better chance of keeping your spending healthy.

Second, to increase the pleasure of buying. There is just something satisfying about waiting until exactly the right moment to purchase. Think about your childhood. How much of your pleasure did you get from the actual birthday gift you got and how much did you get in the waiting for that gift? Daydreaming of what the gift could be, the suspense of it all, the ritual. Random gifts lose their meaning. Gifting as a calendar-based ritual is more pleasurable for most people.

It can be the same for you and your dividends. Most companies pay dividends quarterly; some monthly or yearly. Either way, most companies that do pay dividends strive to maintain a clockwork regularity. This means that you can mark on a calendar, one year in advance, exactly when your pay days will be. Even better than your annual birthday, now your birthday comes four times a year!

The skills you learned as a kid still work today. If you think you are going to get your dividends in the last week of April, then in March you'll start thinking about how best to invest those dividends. Again, you don't need to do this. This reinvestment can be fully automatic if you desire. But many people get pleasure out of the ritual. Just like the expert green thumb that gently clips a vine here or plants a new bush there, you are tending your garden to get to your ultimate goal, except your green thumb is the kind that blossoms dead presidents.

Patient, methodical dividend reinvestment is a great way to get your hands in the soil without becoming a mad day trader. For an investor who generally understands that your involvement in your own investments should be minimal, this is a way to have some fun without taking a chainsaw to your own money garden.

But what if this just isn't enough? You see so many good companies out there: you must buy to capitalize! You see so many bad managers: you must sell to avoid disaster! All of my data, all of my real-world stories, all of my analogies, are a tepid defense against the raging bull that lives inside your head. "Buy!" It screams. "Sell!" It moans. "Data be damned, we need action!"

If you have read this whole book and you still realize that you are the unlucky person who cannot resist the compulsion to buy and sell stocks on a regular basis, I still have one last trick for you. This last technique has worked for even the most hopeless day traders. I know, because it has even worked for me.

Chapter 12: If You Must, Part II (The Gambler)

So far, you have been reading all of my tips and tricks regarding self-discipline and long-term investment, and you'll already have a distinct gut feeling. That gut feeling says either, "Yeah, I can make this work" or "This is never gonna work, I've got to trade. Got to!" If you fall into the first group, just skip this chapter and go on to the next. If you feel the pit of your stomach growling "Must trade ... must ... trade," don't worry, there is still hope for you! Read on.

If you must trade stocks, buying and selling frequently based on news, rumors, or supposed insights you have had, just go right ahead and do it. After all, some forces of nature simply cannot be contained. Just make sure you are gambling at a level you can afford.

I will teach you a specific trick to save you from ruin. It helps to visualize a casino. As we have explored in depth, long-term investing is a game of skill; you need intellectual prowess to pick winning enterprises that will thrive for decades and you need the emotional discipline to hang onto those shares through thick and thin. Buying a stock for a month and selling on a whim becomes a game of chance, just like those in a casino. But casinos are fun. Las Vegas and Macau are some of the largest tourist attractions in the world. Millions of people visit for a casual thrill every year; only a small fraction fall into the corrosive life of a gambling addict. This chapter will teach you how to enjoy it with moderation.

Low Stakes, High Thrills

What if I told you that the amount of money a gambler wagers is often irrelevant? In other words, wagering $10 can be just as exciting as wagering $1000. There are a few reasons for this.

The first reason is that at least 50% of the thrill of gambling is not based on the wager itself, but in the ritual and the pageantry of the casino. Vegas casinos go to extraordinary lengths to create an all-encompassing, 360° sensory experience: flashing lights, sparkling crystal, card dealers wearing special uniforms. There is a certain pulse-accelerating effect merely entering Lady Luck's lair. Then there is the ritual of approaching and seating yourself at the table, looking around and sizing up the other players at the table, picking up a vibe from the card dealer; the feeling of rubbing your fingers over the chips in your hands. Money rarely has such a physical manifestation in our world anymore, so holding it directly in your hand spikes the adrenaline a bit more.

The highly sophisticated corporations that run major casinos know that over 50% of the thrill comes from the overall experience. That is why the lower stakes gambling tables often look just the same as the higher stakes gambling tables, except the super high rollers gamble in their own rooms, which creates an air of exclusivity and makes sure that low stakes gamblers don't accidentally scat themselves with the big gamblers. I know this, because I've done it myself by accident. I thought I was going to the $10 table and instead I wound up at the $100 table. They look just the same. The pageantry, the uniforms, the gamblers themselves. All the same. If the $1000 table hadn't been behind a velvet rope, I may well have wandered over there by accident.

The point is, you can still get a pretty big jolt of adrenaline from low stakes gambling. The other way of thinking about this arrangement is by considering that 'low stakes' could mean something different to everyone. Have you ever read one of those finance articles with a headline that reads: "Jeff Bezos loses $10 billion in one day." Oh my goodness, what is going on with Amazon? Are they somehow suddenly falling behind? Is the online shopping king about to lose his throne? No, the media just loves to play games with math. To 99.99% of humanity, $10 billion is an unfathomable amount of wealth. But to Bezos, it's actually a rounding error. If his holdings of Amazon stock come in at $200 billion, a small fluctuation in the share price could make it look like he 'lost' $10 billion in one day. Is this low stakes poker? Hell no. Is this low stakes poker to Jeff Bezos? Astoundingly, yes.

It's no different for you. If you are truly of modest means, then gambling $10,000 on risky stock trading might feel like a fortune to you. But if you are a mid-career executive and investor with a growing net worth, you might be able to put $100,000 or more into a stock trading portfolio and still only be playing with a manageable percentage of your net worth. This is actually the exact technique that I recommend for the 'must trade' crowd.

Safety First

A Porsche sports car is a speed machine that simply was not built to drive at the speed limit. Show me a Porsche owner who claims that they only drive 65 miles per hour and I will show you a liar. Some people just feel the need to own a dream machine and drive faster than what is prudent because we only live once.

A smart person enjoys their Porsche while taking a few basic precautions. They will wear a seatbelt, they won't drink and drive, they don't take their Porsche over 20 MPH in a school zone.

This is called responsible enjoyment. Well, mostly responsible enjoyment. You can do exactly the same with your stock portfolio.

"If you're going to gamble, be prepared to lose." My uncle, a very accomplished business person, once told me that. That statement has been one of my operating principles for decades. So, if you know yourself and you know that you just can't resist buying and selling stocks, no matter what the data say, you need to first sit down with a spreadsheet and ask yourself the honest answer to this tough question: "How much could I afford to lose without triggering disastrous consequences for my family or my retirement?"

Everyone will have a different answer to that question, but I will help guide you. You absolutely should not be trading stocks with more than 20% of your total net worth. I would really advocate for about 10% of your net worth; enough to give you that thrill you're looking for, but not enough to really damage the golden future that you have worked so hard to build.

One of the greatest elements to this strategy is the fact that the market will evolve with you. In just the last few years, the market has changed to accommodate small investors. It used to be that if you were only trading $1000, or even $10,000, any potential profits would get eaten up by fees. But, now, most people, even at the lowest levels, can trade for free. So, if 10% of your net worth equals $100,000, then put that money aside. If 10% of your net worth equals just $1000, then put that aside. This technique works equally well for Big Shots as well as Aspiring Big Shots.

After this separation, you should have two pots of money. 90% of your money will go into plain, vanilla, conservative index funds and big name 'blue chip' stocks. This is your "slow but steady" portfolio. Choose a brokerage, park the money, and forget that you own it. Read your statements a few times a year. Other than that, ignore this portion of your wealth. This is the portfolio that will really make you rich over time.

Then take your remaining 10% and put that in a separate brokerage. Note, I didn't say a "separate brokerage account." I said, "a separate brokerage." What is the difference?

One individual investor can easily have multiple accounts at the same brokerage. Let's say you have three accounts at E-Trade. When you log into E-Trade, the home screen will show all three accounts next to each other. This is no good! Leaving everything in the same place increases the temptation to trade it all (by the way, the brokerages only make money when you trade, so they do this on purpose to stimulate trading).

Having separate brokerages solves the temptation problem. In this case, perhaps you might put 90% of your assets in plain vanilla index funds with Vanguard and 10% of your assets with Robinhood. That way, you are checking your Robinhood 10 times a week or 10 times a day, but the bulk of your wealth will quietly compound over at Vanguard, year after year, safely out of the limelight.

Human Beings: The Social Animal

Think back to that casino for a minute. How much of the fun and excitement is simply about numbers, odds, and chips and how much is it about other people? Sizing up the other players at the table, trying to read the dealer, reporting and comparing gambling outcomes with friends. People like to win money; but, more importantly, people like other people to know that they won money.

The same thing happens in today's fast-paced stock trading culture. Now that people can trade dozens of times per day from their cell phone and report those trades to friends, family members, or anyone who will listen, huge online communities exist, dedicated exclusively to the 'Fast Money' crowd. These communities exist supposedly because trading is serious business. Hopefully the statistical analysis provided earlier in this book has convinced you that frequent stock trading is, in fact, more like monkey business; it is unlikely to be productive, but is a lot of fun while you're doing it. And, hey, enjoyment needs to be a part of life.

So, now, you are ready for responsible enjoyment. Most of your money is safe in a brokerage account that you rarely check; "Out of sight, out of mind," as the saying goes. You can excuse yourself from a boring meeting at work, go into the bathroom, and use your cell phone to scoop up shares in the latest hot tech IPO. You can post notes on Twitter telling the world about your big score. You can text your WhatsApp chat group to let them know that the High Roller is at it again. Using the 90/10 separation technique, you can enjoy the social and gambling elements of trading, without mortgaging the golden future that you have labored to build.

The idea that people build psychological walls in their lives is well established in pop culture and social science. Bruce Wayne is Batman. Jekyll is Hyde. In post WWII America, many stone cold killers on the battlefield came home to build lives of peaceful suburban normality, never again to discuss what happened on the killing fields of the South Pacific or Europe.

You will build a dual identity for yourself: The Fast Money Wall Street player constantly rearranging his portfolio on his smartphone and the disciplined, judicious, long-term investor, who rarely sells solid blue chip stocks.

But even the judicious, long haul business owner will occasionally need to sell a stock holding. The whole point of this book is to show that you should rarely sell shares. But not never. Nothing in this life is never. There comes a time to sell a business. I will leave you with some critical guidance on this rare event.

Chapter 13: When To Sell

As I've stated dozens of times throughout this book, a successful investor should sell stocks very rarely. However, those rare moments that do emerge are critical. In order to establish a firm framework around the concept, let's return to our dry cleaner analogy from chapter 2.

You and your two siblings own a small dry-cleaning chain. Your Dad started the business decades ago and, through diligence and good fortune, you three siblings have managed to build a local chain of 10 stores. At this point, you have a general manager who does most of the heavy lifting for you; the main tasks of the three owners are to provide high level oversight, high level direction, and count the money that comes in. And the money does come in; quarter after quarter, year after year, for decades on end.

But lately, something has happened. Something new. A friend of yours in the textile business told you about a new kind of fabric technology that means that clothes will rarely need to be cleaned. This new chemical technology means that a shirt could go months without being wrinkled or stained. This is not good for someone who owns a dry-cleaning business.

You do some independent research and find out that this report is true. Although the new fabric technology is just now emerging from the lab, it is possible that in five years or so, the stain-resistant, wrinkle-resistant technology will be worn by millions of people.

You convene a private meeting to discuss the situation with your fellow sibling owners. After much discussion and debate, a division opens up between the three of you. You feel that the value of the business is in grave danger; new clothing with better chemistry means less dry cleaning. Your two siblings think this technology will be just another bump in the road of a lucrative business that has remained almost the same for decades; they want to hold on and attempt to adapt to the change.

So, ⅔ of shareholders don't want to sell the business. Effective control of the business won't change hands. But they do offer to buy you out. Since the business still produces strong cash flow, your sibling partners make you a fair, perhaps even generous, offer. In addition to your serious doubts about the future of the dry-cleaning business, the truth is, you have had your eye on a construction business for a while, which the proceeds could be put towards. After careful thought and some soul searching, you sell out to your sibling partners. This principle and scenario would be similar if you owned ⅓ of a dry-cleaning business or 0.003% of a Fortune 500 company that makes dry cleaning chemicals. A shareholder is a shareholder.

Who got the better deal in the example above? Is it the remaining sibling shareholders, who now have one less shareholder to worry about? Or is it the sibling who liquidated and who now doesn't have to fret about fundamental core changes to the dry-cleaning market? Only time will tell. Two groups of rational people analyzed the situation and came up with two different answers. But the key is, the sale was prompted by fundamental changes in the overall market. You would never sell your shares in a profitable, established business on a whim or a rumor.

Fundamentals, Fundamentals, Fundamentals

As we come to the end of this book, I will leave you with one last Warren Buffett quote. This one is a real zinger.

"Try to invest in a business that an idiot can run. Because, believe me, eventually, an idiot will run it."

With the flick of his sharp tongue, Uncle Warren delivers just as much business knowledge as you might get from a Harvard MBA. In fact, he probably gives you, for free, knowledge that you would never get from a Harvard MBA. This is because Harvard is in the business of charging big bucks to teach people how to manage businesses. How much would they be able to charge if they openly admitted what Buffett already knows? Management hardly matters for a good business.

But how could that be? When we say a 'good' business, we mean one in which the dynamic of supply and demand is in favor of the supplier. There are many reasons why this imbalance may occur and persist, but it's a clear and obvious pattern over time. Successful long-term corporate businesses actually have surprisingly little competition. They sell goods and services that are, for a variety of reasons, scarce. Therefore, they can be run by an idiot and it won't really matter.

Ouch! But think about it. If you're going shopping online, you will likely be using Google to search. Of course, they mint money; they have a 90% market share. You may well buy from Amazon. If you don't like Amazon, perhaps Target or Walmart. But, statistically, you will be buying from the 'Big Three'. All other competitors are minnows next to these three giants.

Even legendary technology upstarts have grown like wildfire and then slowed dramatically as competition emerged. IBM and GE were the high-tech wonder kids of the 60s and 70s. Now? Not so much. I'll let you in on a not-so-little secret. In the 60s and 70s, there was little competition on the global stage. Half of Germany was still occupied by a nightmarish communist regime and the rest of Germany had to live in constant fear of invasion. Japan was just emerging from the smoldering wreckage of WWII. Communist China was known more for starving children than building iPhones. IBM and GE emerged to provide cutting edge technology, in the form of products and services, that few others could provide at the time. Now dozens of different companies from around the world compete to provide similar services. Guess what? Investors who sold IBM and GE decades ago got the better end of the deal.

The growth of Tesla has been a phenomenon for the record books. Elon Musk and his team created a brand new market for electric cars out of thin air. Against long odds, investors have been hugely rewarded with a return on investment. But, up until now, Musk and Co have had virtually no competition. Now that a firm market for the vehicles has been established, everyone and his brother is coming to grab a slice of it. It could get a lot harder from here for Musk. Will he eventually go the way of IBM and GE? Who knows? But the market is changing in a big way.

The number one reason to sell a stock is if there is a major change in the competitive landscape. It doesn't matter what kind of super MBAs you may be employing to run your company. If they suddenly have double or triple the number of competitors and the overall demand for goods and services remains the same, investment returns will be weak for years or decades ahead.

Another reason to sell would be if there was a core change in the demand for a product that has nothing to do with competition. It wasn't great to be in the horse business when Henry Ford introduced the Model T car. This is like our dry-cleaning example.

Another example of this change in underlying demand could be seen in the energy business. About 10 years ago, I sold all of my oil stocks and I bought into Tesla. It just seemed to me that oil was a necessary evil in society, but as that evil became less and less necessary, demand would drop. Tesla, while risky and unproven, seemed to me to be the technology of the future. As of the writing of this text, my prediction has come true. Major oil stocks have struggled for years. As the saying goes, "The stone age didn't end for lack of stone."

Personal Choices about Personnel

If top management hardly matters in your typical Fortune 500 company, would that mean that personnel changes should not be a reason to sell a stock? The not-so-simple answer to that simple question is "it depends."

Financial history is filled with many examples and counterexamples. For example, when Steve Jobs was unceremoniously fired from the company that he founded, it didn't take the corporate dimwits who replaced him very long to run the once-thriving concern directly into the ground. When a desperate board of directors coaxed Jobs to return years later, the company's fortunes began to turn around almost immediately. In this case, the change in management really did matter.

On the other hand, some of the biggest names in Big Pharma have thrived for a hundred years or more with a constant rotation of top executives. Pfizer, Merck, Eli Lilly ... they have ground out profits for decades with such machine-like efficacy that probably the village idiot could probably run the company and still produce a decent return on investment. Ultimately, developing and bringing to market major new pharmaceutical innovations is a very expensive proposition that requires highly specialized knowledge and contacts. About 10 large companies split up a global market of 7,000,000,000 people. That's not a lot of companies serving an almost incomprehensible number of people. The chief executive could probably play golf 7 days a week and still churn out boku bucks for you, the investor.

Perhaps the biggest factor that should be considered is the situation surrounding personnel changes. Mega Corporations, such as Big Pharma, tend to have very well-orchestrated succession plans that are announced well ahead of time. When you are paying an executive $20,000,000 or more each year, and they are a substantial shareholder in the firm, any sudden departure under less than transparent conditions is a major red flag. As we've stated, you can get away with almost anything at the top of Corporate America. If your CEO has just not gotten away with something, you need to investigate the circumstances.

While the CEO that you employ to run your company may or may not be highly competent, they are very likely to be highly ruthless. They have put in decades of 80-hour work weeks to arrive at the pinnacle of Corporate America and demand the same grueling work schedule from their (and your) top executive team. This is great news for you as a passive shareholder. You can sit by the pool with a pina colada because some vice president somewhere is missing his kid's birthday to make more money for the shareholders (you). But sometimes ruthless goes over the line into criminality and corruption. Sometimes way over the line. When this happens, it may be time to sell.

A great example of this is Wells Fargo Bank. Wells Fargo was one of the most established venerable banks in the world. Millions of Americans were touched by Wells Fargo in one way or another. It turns out, millions of Americans were also screwed raw by the very same Wells Fargo.

The saying "A fish rots from the head down" was true for Wells Fargo. After a storied career climbing the corporate ladder of major American banks, John Stumpf, MBA, was promoted to the role of President of Well Fargo in 2005. Within a few years, he had consolidated his power over the giant bank, achieving the title of Chairman and CEO. Stumpf proceeded to build one of the largest fraud machines the world has ever seen. Subsequent investigations by the SEC, the United States Congress, and just about every other governmental agency, concluded that Stumpf and his team had methodically required associates to fabricate accounts and create millions of credit card accounts that no one had asked for. The response from the Board of Directors was to fire Stumpf and promote his Chief Operating Officer, the very same executive who had partnered with Stumpf for years in the creation of his fraud machine. Of course, this didn't go over well with the media, investors, or the legions of government investigators who proceeded to nail Wells Fargo to the cross. Investors lost billions in fines. Investigations are still ongoing today, 5 years after the fraud was uncovered.

From Stumpf's appointment as President in 2005, through the Great Financial Crisis, to the eve of his downfall, the executive produced a 150% total return for investors. That is a stellar number for a classic, slow growth S&P 500 behemoth. If investors had sold at the first hint of corruption, they would have walked away in good shape. Subsequently, poor Wells Fargo has still not recovered. From 2016 to August 2020, the shares produced a cumulative return of -44%. Just for comparison, Apple produced a return of +450% during that period. In this example, leadership mattered!

You'll have to make your own judgements about leadership and leadership changes in the companies you own.

Think about it just as if you owned that dry cleaning chain and you were hiring or firing a general manager.

So, the three main reasons to sell a stock are:

-Meaningful change in a competitive market place
-Meaningful technological and societal change that transforms a market.
-Abrupt or suspicious leadership change.

Tuning Out The Dumb Dumbs

About 95% of the time, the three reasons listed above are the only reasons to sell a long-term stock holding. However, there are all kinds of people who claim to see all kinds of signs and portents that will supposedly allow them to predict outcomes. Most of these analysts are about as reliable as a gypsy palm reader.

Do NOT sell a stock based on an analyst's recommendations. You should be your own analyst. You may choose to watch an analyst interviewed on CNBC or Bloomberg, but this is mostly for entertainment and to get your own ideas flowing. You may occasionally choose to read analyst reports if you get them for free through your brokerage. But mostly, analysts are just people with the very same human limitations as everybody else. They may have more formal education than you, as we have discussed, but some of that education may actually be a liability in terms of accuracy.

Do NOT sell a stock based on chart patterns that some trading 'expert' swears will predict the future. You may have heard terms such as 'support levels', 'golden cross', or 'momentum breakthrough'. These are simply Wall Street translations of the old incantations, 'Hocus', 'Pocus', 'Dominocus'. If it sounds like nonsense, that's because it is nonsense.

Do NOT sell a stock because the company has faced a temporary setback. We have already discussed examples of fundamental problems. These are actually somewhat rare, which is why S&P 500 companies tend to churn out cash decade after decade. An example of a temporary setback would be: A big pharma company suffering a failure in a clinical trial; a car company with a poorly selling new model, a Hollywood studio that releases a bomb of a film.

In all three of these examples, the company has temporarily underperformed. However, these failures do not necessarily indicate an overall failure of the business model. If a Hollywood studio is constantly birthing still-born movies, then there may be something systematically wrong. But a certain amount of episodic failure is just part of business, even big business. Ultimately, there just aren't that many entities out there that have the massive capital base, deep knowledge, and contacts to create and distribute major motion pictures. Most studios can easily shrug off a dud and move on. Instead of you selling shares at a temporary low point, you might actually want to consider buying more.

Money Mind

Ultimately, human beings live in a world shaped and formed by our psychology. Societal ideas that are widespread become accepted as objective facts. People have worked themselves to the bone for money. They have crossed oceans, dug mines, and even harnessed the powers of nature for money. Sadly, many have even killed for money. All for some little green pieces of paper!

The architecture of our mind makes things real or not real. The goal of this book has been to help you draw a mental blueprint that will result in a solid financial house. I already know that you are smart enough, because you don't have to be very smart. I already know that you are educated enough, because you don't have to be very educated. I already know that you have enough money to get started, because you don't need much money to get started.

The real questions are:
"Are you disciplined enough?"
"Are you focused enough?"
"Are you ready to become the master of your own emotions?"

Saying "YES!" to these three questions will help you to build your Money Mind. The very same Money Mind that will put real money in your pocket.

Other Works by The Sick Economist

Your First Biotech Million: How to Earn Your Fortune in Biotech Stocks

Read the latest analysis and commentary about biotech investing and sign up for our free newsletter, The Rx, at www.SickEconomics.com